Ibiza
& Formentera
DIRECTIONS

WRITTEN AND RESEARCHED BY

Iain Stewart

NEW YORK • LONDON • DELHI
www.roughguides.com

Contents

Introduction to

Ibiza
& Formentera

After decades of negative publicity that branded the island as little more than a budget-level ravers' paradise, Ibiza is rapidly reasserting itself as one of Spain's most cosmopolitan corners – an affluent, self-confident island with a fascinating heritage and a vibrant, home-grown music and fashion scene of global reach and importance.

A pivotal part of the Carthaginian empire between 600 and 50 BC, Ibiza was closely linked with the fertility goddess Tanit and the god of dance Bes (from whom the name Ibiza is derived). Its status, however, quickly waned under Roman occupation, and the island remained a backwater for two thousand years until the early 1960s when political opponents of Franco settled here and waves of beatniks discovered the island. Ibiza's decidedly bohemian character is rooted in this era, and continues

When to visit

Ibiza and Formentera are very warm between June and late September when cloudless skies are virtually guaranteed. The heat can get intense in July and August, when highs in the 30s are common, but even at this time of year cooling sea breezes usually intervene to prevent things getting too uncomfortable. Winter in the Pitiuses is also glorious, with very little rainfall and temperatures ordinarily high enough to enjoy sitting outside in cafés, even in January. As far as crowds go, there's a very clearly defined tourist season on both islands that begins slowly in early May, peaks in August when the islands get really packed, and slowly winds down throughout September. The last charter flights leave at the end of October. Winter is a wonderfully peaceful time for a visit, but flight connections are thin on the ground and there's little in the way of nightlife.

▲ *Amnesia*

to be particularly strong in the north of the island, where you'll find yoga retreats, ethnic bazaars and a large population of alternative thinkers.

The island's natural beauty is captivating. Large swathes of the coastline survive in pristine condition, with sweeping sandy bays and exquisite coves tucked beneath soaring cliffs. Ibiza's hilly, thickly wooded interior is peppered with isolated white-washed villages and terraced fields of almonds, figs and olives. The charismatic capital, Ibiza Town, harbours most of the island's architectural treats, including a spectacular walled enclave, Dalt Vila, and a port area replete with hip bars, stylish

◀ Coastline near Cala Moli

Language

Catalan is replacing Castilian Spanish as the official language of the islands, and we have therefore used Catalan names throughout the guide.

restaurants and fashionable boutiques. Laying claim to be the world's clubbing capital, Ibiza is an incredibly hedonistic place, where the nights are celebrated with unique spirit in landmark clubs scattered across the island.

Serene, easy-going Formentera, the other main island of the Pitiuses (southern Balearics), is just a short ferry ride south of Ibiza and yet a complete contrast. Boasting a relaxed, unhurried atmosphere and miles of ravishing sandy beaches lapped by translucent water, it has little or no nightlife and few historical sights apart from some sombre fortress churches and minor archeological ruins.

▲ Ibiza Town harbour

Ibiza & Formentera
AT A GLANCE

Ibiza Town

Sassy Ibiza Town, the vibrant island capital, is one of the most scenic ports in the Mediterranean. The colossal medieval walls of its old *barrio*, Dalt Vila (a UNESCO World Heritage Site), provide a startlingly evocative backdrop and contain most of Ibiza's historic buildings, including the castle and cathedral.

▲ Dalt Vila

Sant Antoni

Offering enough bars in the West End zone to drown the devil himself, as well as the clubbing meccas of *Eden* and *Es Paradis*, and the stylish chillout bars of the Sunset Strip, unpretentious Sant Antoni draws young clubbers in droves.

▼ Carrer Sant Vicent

◄ Sant Antoni sunset

Santa Eulària

This agreeable seaside town hosts an attractive marina and a historic hilltop quarter. Tuck into tapas on its famous street of restaurants, Carrer Sant Vicent.

Northern Ibiza

Northern Ibiza is the least populated part of the island, its countryside a mix of rust-red terraced fields interspersed by diminutive villages and dense pine-forested peaks. Little development mars a coastline of isolated coves, rugged cliffs and lonely stone watchtowers – a hiker's delight.

▼ Cala Llentrisca

▲ s'Illot des Renclí

Southern Ibiza

Endowed with over a dozen bite-shaped *calas* (coves), the shimmering Salines salt flats and the remarkable soaring offshore islet of Es Vedrà, southern Ibiza's coastline is extraordinarily beguiling.

▼ Espalmador

Formentera

The island of Formentera, comprising two flat promontories linked by a narrow sandy isthmus, is very thinly populated, much less developed than Ibiza and boasts stunning beaches surrounded by crystalline waters.

Ideas

The big six

Ibiza is rightly renowned for its nightlife but the island also has a seductive beauty that begs exploration. Shaping up at just 50km by 18km, nowhere is more than an hour's drive away, while much smaller Formentera stretches only 15km from west to east. As well as almost innumerable cove beaches, the islands offer a fascinatingly diverse range of sights, from glistening bird-rich salt flats and soaring craggy cliffs to tranquil, architecturally historic villages.

▼ Salines saltpans

Both Ibiza and Formentera boast extensive salt flats, glittering pools of seawater that were first developed for salt production by the Phoenicians.

P.139 ▸ THE SOUTH
P.154 ▸ FORMENTERA

▼ Port area at night

There's a real buzz to Ibiza Town's port on summer nights, when it's the perfect place for some early evening retail therapy, followed by an atmospheric alfresco dinner and, for those that have the stamina, the mother of all bar crawls.

P.51 ▸ IBIZA TOWN

◀ Dalt Vila

Forming one of Europe's best-preserved walled cities, UNESCO World Heritage-listed Dalt Vila is richly atmospheric and contains the island's top historical attractions.

▶ Clubbing

As house music's spiritual home, Ibiza serves up a selection of the globe's leading DJs virtually every night of the week in the summer months.

◀ Platja Illetes

The finest beach in the southern Balearics, this sublime slender finger of white sand lapped by shallow pellucid waters lies at Formentera's northern tip.

▶ Es Vedrà

Looming above the southern coastline, this enigmatic 378-metre-high offshore island looks magnificent from any angle.

Rural bliss

Nothing beats waking up to a view from your bedroom over fields of olive and almond trees stretching to pine-forested hills.

Ibiza's rural hotel sector is booming, and there are plenty of terrific places to stay in all corners of the island. Most are converted farmhouses, extremely comfortable and stylishly decorated, and because the island is so small, it's easy to stay somewhere quite remote and still be close to the action.

▲ Can Lluc

Seriously swanky *agroturismo* hotel, with elegant, stylish rooms and a huge swimming pool.

P.120 ▸ SANT ANTONI

▲ Can Pere

Classy, stylish and very well run, this small, welcoming hotel enjoys extensive grounds and wonderful views of Ibiza's central hills.

P.89 ▸ THE EAST

▲ Can Martl

Close to the village of Sant Joan, this tranquil rustic place is set on a working organic farm and is great value for money.

▶ Es Cucons

This highly popular, luxuriously converted farmhouse is set in Ibiza's unspoiled western hills and combines rural character with all mod cons.

▼ Can Talaias

Wonderful country retreat, high on a hill with jaw-dropping views over Ibiza's eastern coast.

Clubs

Ibiza is home to a clutch of the planet's most celebrated club venues and the scene is potent enough to break new tunes and influence dance floors all over the world. A who's who of the world's leading house DJs play here in the summer season, when the atmosphere in the clubs can approach almost devotional intensity.

▲ Pacha

More than just a club, Ibiza Town's *Pacha* is the base of a global entertainment empire, regularly hosting the world's leading DJs. It also contains one of clubland's most elegant and enjoyable chillout terraces.

P.78 ▶ IBIZA TOWN

▲ El Divino

A glamourous harbourside club, *El Divino* is gaining a reputation for its signature vocal house nights.

P.77 ▶ IBIZA TOWN

▼ Privilege

This venue – the biggest in the world and the home of Manumission – is quite extraordinary, housing a huge main arena complete with swimming pool, the *Coco Loco* (club-within-a-club) and a back room which hosts live music.

P.127 ▶ SANT ANTONI

▼ DC10

Serving up pure mayhem every Monday, *DC10* draws Europe's party hardcore; some of the most acclaimed DJs have begged to play here for free.

P.144 ▶ THE SOUTH

▲ Amnesia

Birthplace of the Balearic Beat and the subsequent Acid house phenomenon, *Amnesia* today has some fearsome techno and trance nights and the best gay party in Ibiza.

P.125 ▶ SANT ANTONI

▲ Space

Twice voted the world's best club at the Dancestar awards, *Space* hosts a legendary Sunday session on its terrace.

P.143 ▶ THE SOUTH

Kids' Ibiza

Ibizans and Formenterans are extremely accommodating towards children, who are welcome in virtually all restaurants. With dozens of fine beaches and warm seas most of the year, children will be easily pleased. All of the family-oriented beaches have umbrellas and pedalos for hire, and most offer banana-boat trips for a speedy thrill.

▼ Beach fun

Pedal-powered floats are available for rent at every family-oriented beach in Ibiza, or for more of a thrill, ride the waves with an inflatable yellow fruit between your legs.

P.168 ▸ ESSENTIALS

▼ Go-karting

Test your boy-racer skills at one of Ibiza two go-kart tracks, located on the Ibiza Town–Santa Eulària road and just outside Sant Antoni.

P.170 ▸ ESSENTIALS

▲ Talamanca

The best beach within walking distance of Ibiza Town, Talamanca has shallow turquoise water, an arc of fine sand, and a good restaurant or two.

P.63 ▸ IBIZA TOWN

▼ Aguamar

Waterworld extravaganza with a serpentine collection of chutes and slides, sure to bring a smile to the most jaded child (or adult).

P.138 ▸ THE SOUTH

Sunsets

Sunset watching is taken very seriously in Ibiza. Join the crowds at a stylish chillout bar where all chairs face west and you can sip a cocktail while taking in a blood-red Balearic sundown to a DJ's mix of emotive music, or for something less commercialized, there are plenty of beautiful bays offering a more peaceful visual experience.

▼ Es Vedrà

Es Vedrà looks majestic at any time of day, but around sunset, purple and crimson hues give this island a hypnotic allure.

P.132 ▸ THE SOUTH

▲ Café Mambo

The crowds here confirm that this bar is one of the most hyped places on the planet to take in a sunset, but at least you're guaranteed a mighty DJ mix to match the scene.

P.124 ▶ SANT ANTONI

▼ Cala Saona

A terrific place in Formentera to catch the sun setting into the ocean, the pink horizon shared with the craggy outlines of distant Ibiza and Es Vedrà.

P.150 ▶ FORMENTERA

▼ Benirràs

Join the drummers at northern Ibiza's drop-dead gorgeous cove beach to celebrate the spectacular Sunday sundown.

P.98 ▶ THE NORTHWEST

▲ Cala Salada

On winter days the islands opposite this bay create a perfect frame for a scarlet sunset.

P.117 ▶ SANT ANTONI

Shopping

Ibiza Town's port zone has dozens of zany boutiques selling everything from bargain-priced accessories to oh-so-hip club- and beach-wear, with all the main designer labels well represented. Don't miss out on the quirky charm of Las Dalias if you're after anything with an ethnic flavour, and if you can't get that tune out of your head you'll find CD and vinyl specialists in Ibiza Town and Sant Antoni.

▲ Beachwear stalls

Many beaches – including Sa Caleta and Calines – have a market stall or two selling a great selection of sarongs and swimwear.

P.136 & P.138 ▸ THE SOUTH

▼ El Secreto de Baltasar

Ibiza Town's most stylish shoe store, with hip footwear for men and women at affordable prices.

P.69 ▶ IBIZA TOWN

▼ Las Dalias market

All things Oriental – from Moroccan rugs to hubble-bubble pipes – in one of Ibiza's most quirky markets.

P.92 ▶ THE EAST

▲ Casi Todo auction house

From rustic farmhouse tables to rusty mountain bikes, this Santa Gertrudis auction house is a snooper's delight.

P.102 ▶ THE NORTHWEST

▲ Plastic Fantastic

A turntablist's mecca, San An's Plastic Fantastic is the perfect place to pick 'n' mix your tunes.

P.121 ▶ SANT ANTONI

Dine in style

From Asian fusion and Provençal restaurants to wave-side seafood *chiringuitos* and wonderful rural retreats serving charcoal-grilled island-reared meat, Ibiza hosts a real diversity of places to eat. Dalt Vila's many pavement-terrace restaurants offer a fantastically evocative setting, but elsewhere many of the best places are off the beaten track – up a country lane or at the end of a potholed track. There's less choice on Formentera, but you'll find some great fish restaurants. Finish your meal with a shot of Hierbas liqueur or a Sa Caleta coffee.

▼ El Boldado

Wonderful spot for paella, seafood or a steak, high above Cala d'Hort with views across to Es Vedrà.

P.141 ▶ THE SOUTH

▼ Gusto

Ibiza's most most modern, metropolitan-style cuisine, in a restaurant that retains a sociable, and friendly vibe.

P.72 ▶ IBIZA TOWN

▼ El Bigotes

The perfect setting for an informal but memorable seafood lunch, right by the water's edge.

P.91 ▶ THE EAST

▲ Pasajeros

Diminutive diner with terrific budget-priced Mediterranean food that's popular with a hip clubland crowd.

P.72 ▶ IBIZA TOWN

▼ Bambuddha Grove

Stunning restaurant and bar built by Balinese craftsmen and serving (mainly) Asian cuisine.

P.106 ▶ THE NORTHWEST

Port bars

Ibiza Town's riotous high-season port bar scene is founded on Spanish sociability, with added spice injected by the hordes of international party-goers that jet in each year. Grab a terrace seat for a ringside view of the theatrical club parades of costumed dancers that wind through the port's streets around midnight. The cavern-like bars on and around c/de la Verge have an underground, alternative feel and many of their owners are happy to advise on the best clubbing action and can often provide guest passes.

▼ Base Bar

A British clubbers' hangout, *Base*'s harbourfront terrace is rammed most nights though the service remains prompt and amiable.

P.73 ▸ IBIZA TOWN

▼ Can Pou Bar

With moderate bar prices for this area, *Can Pou* is an atmospheric place that has a loyal (mainly) local clientele, and it's also open all year.

P.74 ▸ IBIZA TOWN

▲ Bar Zuka

An intimate, modish drinking den, this is the only straight bar on Ibiza's main gay street.

P.73 ▶ IBIZA TOWN

▼ Mao Rooms

Oriental fabrics, velvet drapes and lounge beds adorn this hip bar, which pulls in a fashion-conscious metropolitan crowd.

P.74 ▶ IBIZA TOWN

Dalt Vila

A focal point for the whole island with floodlit bastions and walls visible for miles around, Dalt Vila ("high town") is the hilltop above the capital, first settled by Phoenicans and later occupied by a wealth of subsequent civilizations. Elegant and tranquil, most of its cobbled lanes are only passable by foot. Enter via the Portal de las Taules gateway and wind your way uphill, as all lanes lead to the cathedral-topped summit.

▲ Cathedral

Striking thirteenth-century Catalan Gothic structure with an impressive bell tower.

P.59 ▶ IBIZA TOWN

▲ Portal de ses Taules

A striking Renaissance-era gateway, this is the grand main entrance into Dalt Vila.

P.57 ▶ IBIZA TOWN

▶ Dining out

The many restaurant terraces make a historic setting for a memorable meal.

P.70 ▶ IBIZA TOWN

▼ Museu d'Art Contemporani

This small contemporary art museum is well worth a visit and all the work has an Ibiza connection.

P.58 ▶ IBIZA TOWN

Alternative Ibiza and Formentera

The islands' bohemian credentials are ubiquitous. Already havens for leftists opposed to Franco, American draft dodgers fleeing the call-up for the Korean and Vietnam wars flocked to the islands in the 1950s and 1960s. This countercultural tendency, including a liberal local attitude towards drug taking, sexuality, green issues and alternative thinking, endures.

▼ Hippodrome market

Ibiza's huge Saturday flea market is a great place to root around for vintage clothes and people-watch.

P.137 ▶ THE SOUTH

▲ Sa Penya boutiques

Kinky and kitsch, hip and happening, the boutiques on c/de la Verge stock what other stores don't or won't.

P.53 ▸ IBIZA TOWN

▲ Aigües Blanques

One of north Ibiza's finest beaches, popular with hippies and costume-free bathers.

P.87 ▸ THE NORTHWEST

◀ Can Sort organic market

Tricky to find, but this Saturday market has select organic produce from Ibiza, and beyond.

P.97 ▸ THE NORTHWEST

▶ Punta de Sa Galera

This small bay, also known as Cala Yoga, has flat rocky shelves ideal for sunbathing as well as more spiritual exercise.

P.117 ▸ SANT ANTONI

Formentera's beaches

Dubbed "the last Mediterranean paradise" by the tourist board – and for once the hyperbole is justified. Formentera's beautiful, sweeping sandy beaches are bordered by a sea of exceptional clarity, and its tiny population and limited tourist development means that things never get too crowded here.

▲ s'Alga, Espalmador

Exquisite sheltered cove beach, with shallow, turquoise-tinged water.

P.154 ▸ FORMENTERA

▲ Platja Illetes

A slender sandbar which stretches north towards Espalmador island, Formentera's finest beach is simply breathtaking from any angle.

P.154 ▸ FORMENTERA

▲ Es Pujols

Magnificent sandy beach, relatively unaffected by the hotel infrastructure of the surrounding resort.

P.152 ▸ FORMENTERA

▼ Cala Saona

Fine cove beach with memorable sunset views from its fringes.

P.150 ▸ FORMENTERA

Village churches

Ibiza and Formentera have an incredible collection of rural churches, with every village boasting a dazzling whitewashed place of worship. Simple, almost minimalist in form, their design (of Moorish origin) influenced Le Corbusier, the celebrated father of Modernist architecture. Most church interiors are stark and relatively unadorned – Republican troops angered by the Catholic Church's support for Franco torched most of their contents in the Civil War.

▼ Sant Miquel

Commanding a magnificent position above the village, the Església de Sant Miquel contains some elaborate frescoes.

P.98 ▶ THE NORTHWEST

▼ El Pilar de la Mola

Its design reminiscent of Ibizan churches, this simple Formenteran whitewashed structure dates from the eighteenth century.

P.157 ▶ FORMENTERA

▲ Jesús

The Nostra Mare de Jesús dates back to the fifteenth century, and has Ibiza's most impressive altar painting.

P.64 ▸ IBIZA TOWN

▼ Sant Carles

An archetypal Ibizan design, with white-washed walls and wonderfully simple lines.

P.84 ▸ THE EAST

▲ Sant Jordi

An unexpected find in a mundane suburb, the unusual Església de Sant Jordi is topped with full battlements.

P.137 ▸ THE SOUTH

▼ Sant Josep

The soaring white facade, complete with sundial, of the substantial Església de Sant Josep is best admired from the village plaza opposite.

P.128 ▸ THE SOUTH

Deserted coves

Because Ibiza and Formentera are so thinly populated, with a combined population of just over 100,000, it's easy to escape the crowds, even in July and August. To get to some of the finest cove beaches – bite-shaped pebble bays between soaring cliffs and sheltered sandy inlets – you'll need to negotiate some rough dirt roads (and often hike along coastal paths).

▲ **s'Estanyol**

Attractive little sandy cove beach, close to Ibiza Town, with great food available in the shoreside *chiringuito*.

P.64 ▶ IBIZA TOWN

▼ Cala d'en Serra

Barely a niche in the coastline, this little beach has a good *chiringuito* for drinks and meals.

▲ Sòl d'en Serra

Quiet bay that's just a short walk from the resort of Cala Llonga, and with a restaurant above the pebble beach.

▼ Cala Llentrisca

Tranquillity is assured at this tiny, remote and beautiful cove.

▲ Platja Codolar

Impressive expanse of wave-polished stones and barely a soul in sight.

Gay Ibiza

Ibiza has been one of Europe's main gay destinations since the 1960s, although the lesbian scene is very limited. Ibiza Town has a gay quarter with bars, a club, and dozens of gay-owned stores and restaurants and the island also offers a stunning beach that is popular with gay men. Most gay visitors stay in either Ibiza Town or Figueretes.

▼ Es Cavallet beach

Arguably the finest beach in southern Ibiza, the gay zone has the best stretch of sand, as well as the wonderful *Chiringay* restaurant.

P.139 ▶ THE SOUTH

La Troya Asesina

Perhaps the best gay club night in Spain, held at *Amnesia* and simply not to be missed.

P.125 ▸ SANT ANTONI

Dôme

The *grande dame* of the gay bar scene – head here to catch the club parades around 1am.

P.76 ▸ IBIZA TOWN

▼ Carrer de la Verge

The heart of Ibiza's gay village, a historic portside street full of gay-owned businesses and bars.

P.56 ▸ IBIZA TOWN

▼ Oriental bar

Super-stylish gay bar with a prime-time location for the club parades, and one of the most enjoyable terraces in town.

P.76 ▸ IBIZA TOWN

Hippy heritage

In the 1960s and 1970s Ibiza and Formentera were one of Europe's key hippy destinations, drawing bohemian folk from all over the world, including musicians Pink Floyd (who recorded *More* in Formentera), Bob Dylan and King Crimson. Relations between the *peluts* ("hairies") and locals were generally good, but there were regular bust-ups with the Guardia Civil over drug use and nudity. Many hippies never left the island, settling in the north of Ibiza around San Joan and in La Mola in Formentera.

▲ Yoga retreats

The practice of yoga has been popular in Ibiza since the 1960s, and the island now has two good Ashtanga retreats.

P.171 ▶ ESSENTIALS

▼ Benirràs beach

Ibiza hippydom's favourite beach – many folk gather here around sunset near the small *chiringuito* at the far end of the bay.

P.98 ▸ THE NORTHWEST

▼ Atlantis

Near-mythical cove, housing an ancient quarry whose rock face has been carved with cosmic imagery.

P.133 ▸ THE SOUTH

▲ Sant Joan

This village is northern Ibiza's main bohemian stronghold; the June fiesta even has a psychedelic trance sound system.

P.93 ▸ THE NORTHWEST

▲ Formentera's windmills

Bob Dylan is said to have lived in a windmill outside La Mola, while the Pink Floyd album *More* features another on its cover.

P.157 ▸ FORMENTERA

Hiking

Ibiza and Formentera are terrific places to hike, with some beautiful country walks past fields of wildflowers and through diminutive villages. It's the coastal hikes, however, that really stand out, offering wonderful views over the Mediterranean. Low annual rainfall and mild, sunny winters mean walking is an option year-round and superb outside the main tourist season.

▼ South of Platja d'en Bossa

Lovely hike on a thickly wooded coastal path, leading to the southernmost point in Ibiza. .

P.137 ▸ THE SOUTH

▼ Up Sa Talaiassa

It's a steep hour (or so) ascent from the village of Sant Josep to Ibiza's highest peak, for panoramic views of the island.

P.129 ▸ THE SOUTH

▲ To Portitxol

Magical path that loops around a lonely part of the northern coast to a stunning rocky cove.

P.100 ▸ THE NORTHWEST

▼ To Atlantis

From the watchtower of Torre des Savinar it's a terrific, if steep, hike down to the old coastal quarry known as Atlantis.

P.133 ▸ THE SOUTH

Off the beaten track

Armed with a map, it's surprisingly easy to really get off the beaten track in Ibiza and Formentera, and there are some wild and pristine landscapes to enjoy. Staking the coast like sentinels are a chain of barely visited stone watchtowers that would have been manned night and day in centuries past, while isolated bays such as the magnificent Cala d'Aubarca are tricky to find but rarely visited by anyone.

▲ Torre des Savinar

High in the southern coastal cliffs opposite Es Vedrà, this is the most evocatively situated of all the islands' old stone defence towers.

P.133 ▶ THE SOUTH

▲ Estany des Peix

The rocky land around the western fringes of Formentera's "lake of fish" has a desolate beauty.

P.146 ▶ FORMENTERA

▲ Cala d'Aubarca

The descent to one of the wildest, most isolated corners of Ibiza has to be done by foot.

▼ Cap de Barbària

Windswept and bleak, Formentera's Barbària peninsula is at its most stirring around its southern tip.

Historic Ibiza and Formentera

Ibiza and Formentera may not offer world-class historical sights, but there are plenty of curious buildings and places of interest, including a vast necropolis, cave shrines and fortified churches.

▼ Puig des Molins

Explore the tombs of this 4000-year-old Punic necropolis, situated in the heart of Ibiza Town.

P.62 ▶ IBIZA TOWN

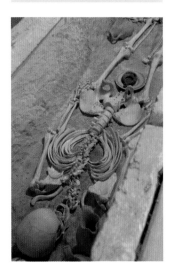

▼ Defence towers

These iconic conical structures define the coast of the Pitiuses islands.

P.87 ▶ THE EAST

▲ Dalt Vila's walls

These mighty foreboding walls were never breached by pirates, and have survived in perfect condition.

P.57 ▸ IBIZA TOWN

▼ Església de Sant Antoni

Once topped with cannons, Sant Antoni's fine fortified church is hidden in the back-streets of town.

P.57 ▸ SANT ANTONI

Ibizan architecture

The Pitiuses' vernacular architecture, particularly the flat-roofed, whitewashed country house known as a *casament*, has been much admired for its simplicity of form. Consisting of a group of interlocking cube-shaped rooms, characteristic details include the triangular chimney openings, the upper balconies (which would have functioned as drying lofts for peppers and herbs) the metre-thick walls and the fine porches which extend outwards from the main body of the house and always face south.

▼ Puig de Missa

This hilltop is the historic heart of Santa Eulària and contains a number of fine period houses, a museum and the town's main church.

P.81 ▶ THE EAST

▼ Es Trui de Can Andreu

A fine old country house, open to the public, just outside Sant Carles.

P.85 ▸ THE EAST

▲ Balàfia

A hamlet with an unusual group of interconnected houses, some with conical defence towers.

P.97 ▸ THE NORTHWEST

▼ Can Berri

This historic village *casament* provides a fantastic setting for a meal.

P.141 ▸ THE SOUTH

▲ Església Santa Agnès de Corona

Whitewashed and with an exterior almost devoid of detail, the simplicity of design of this village church is its trump card.

P.102 ▸ THE NORTHWEST

Places

Ibiza Town and around

Urbane Ibiza Town (Eivissa) is the cultural and admini-
strative heart of the island. Set around a dazzling natural
harbour, it's one of the Mediterranean's most charismatic
pocket-sized capitals, full of hip boutiques, chic bars and
restaurants. In the summer months, its narrow whitewashed lanes become an alfresco catwalk, as a good
selection of the planet's most committed party people
strut the streets in a frenzy of competitive hedonism.
Looming above the port is historic Dalt Vila, a rocky
escarpment topped by a walled enclave, squabbled
over by all the island's invaders since the days of the
Phoenicians. The fortress-like Catalan cathedral and
craggy Moorish castle that bestride the summit are Ibiza's
most famous landmarks, visible across much of the south
of the island. Below Dalt Vila, Ibiza Town's harbour is the
island's busiest, its azure waters ruffled by a succession
of yachts, container ships and ferries. To the west is the
New Town, only really attractive in the streets close to
boulevard-like Vara de Rey; while, occupying the north
side of the bay, the New Harbour zone is an upmarket
pleasure strip. Around Ibiza Town you'll find a couple of
beaches of varying quality and some good café-bars in
the village of Jesús.

La Marina

La Marina, Ibiza Town's
atmospheric harbourside district,
often just referred to as "the
port", is the heart of the Ibizan
capital. A crooked warren of
narrow streets, it's sandwiched
between the harbour waters to
the north and the walls of Dalt
Vila and district of Sa Penya in
the south. Its alleys and tiny plazas
are crammed with fashionable
stores, restaurants and bars, and
the almost souk-like streets fizz
with life until the early hours
during high season. By the end

Arrival and information

Ibiza Town has a small, scruffy bus ticket office on Avgda d'Isidor Macabich; **buses**
stop outside as there's no bus station. Routes and times to all destinations are
included in the relevant entries in the text. **Boats** (all May–Oct only) dock on the
south side of the harbour for a number of destinations including Talamanca, Platja
d'en Bossa and Santa Eulària. All boats to Formentera leave from a terminal on
Avgda Santa Eulària, on the west side of the harbour.

Ibiza Town's efficient **tourist information** office is located opposite the Estació
Marítima (port building) on the Passeig Marítim harbourfront (June–Sept Mon–Fri
8.30am–2.30pm & 5–7pm, Sat 9.30am–1.30pm; Oct–May Mon–Fri 8.30am–
2.30pm; ☎971 301 900).

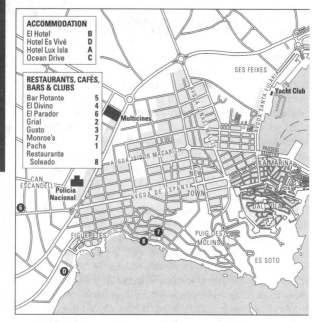

ACCOMMODATION

El Hotel	B
Hotel Es Vivé	D
Hotel Lux Isla	A
Ocean Drive	C

RESTAURANTS, CAFÉS, BARS & CLUBS

Bar Flotante	5
El Divino	4
El Parador	6
Grial	2
Gusto	3
Monroe's	7
Pacha	1
Restaurante Soleado	8

of September, however, the pace abates and most of the restaurants and bars shut up shop.

Along Passeig Marítim

The best place to start exploring La Marina is at the southwestern corner of the harbourfront, along Passeig Marítim. Heading east, a cluster of upmarket café-bars (try *Mar y Sol*) afford fine vistas of the yachts and docks. Past the midway point, marked by the modern harbour building, the Estació Marítima, the street is lined with restaurants and bars. These venues provide an ideal standpoint for taking in the outrageous club parades that are such a feature of the Ibizan night in high season: processions of body-painted and costumed PR people and drag queens promoting events at the big club venues. Further along, the

tiny **Plaça de sa Riba**, backed by tottering old whitewashed fishermen's houses, makes an agreeable place for outdoor

▼LA MARINA AND DALT VILA

dining. At the very end of the *passeig*, the breakwater of Es Muro extends into the harbour, offering an excellent view back over the old town, and a flight of steps heads south up into Sa Penya (see below).

Església Sant Elm

Open only for mass. The Església de Sant Elm, burnt down at least a dozen times by pirates, was first built in the fifteenth century. A sturdy, three-storey, functional design with a tiered bell tower, the present building was constructed after the last church was destroyed during the Spanish Civil War. The cool interior is home to the shell of a giant clam (which doubles as the church font) and a striking statue of a beaming open-armed Christ, complete with 1960s-style hairdo. The other image of interest is the haloed Verge

del Carmen, carrying a child, which has long been associated with the Ibizan seamen's guild and the July 16 fiesta (see p.172).

Plaça de sa Constitució

This small, peaceful square of elegant whitewashed and ochre-painted old merchants' houses is home to Es Mercat Vell (The Old Market), a curiously squat Neoclassical edifice where fruit and vegetables have been traded since 1873. The square is a great place for a refuelling stop before the steep assault on Dalt Vila through the looming presence of the Portal de ses Taules gateway. The most renowned café here is the ever-popular, if chaotic *Croissant Show* (see p.69).

Sa Penya

Sa Penya comprises a twisted triangle of streets hemmed in

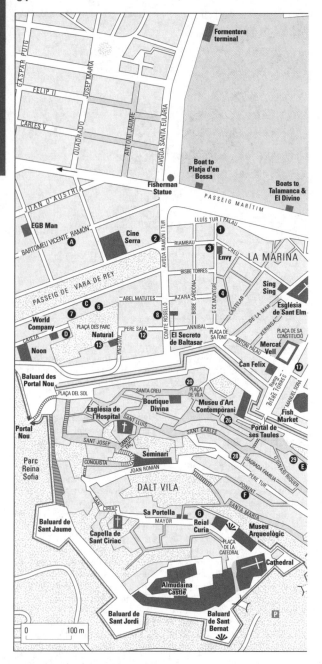

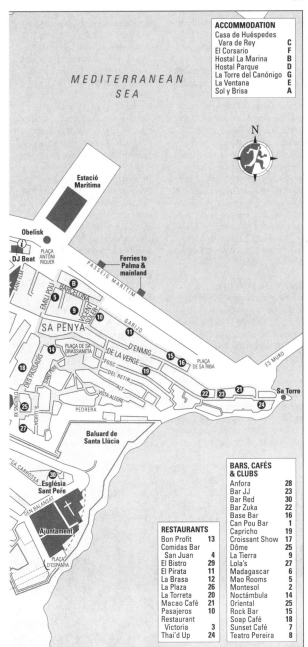

ACCOMMODATION

Casa de Huéspedes Vara de Rey	C
El Corsario	F
Hostal La Marina	B
Hostal Parque	D
La Torre del Canónigo	G
La Ventana	E
Sol y Brisa	A

MEDITERRANEAN SEA

N

Estació Marítima

Obelisk

DJ Beat

PLAÇA ANTÒNI RIQUER

Ferries to Palma & mainland

PASSEIG MARÍTIM

SANT ELM

EMILI POU

BARCELONA

VICENT SOLER

GARIJO

SA PENYA

D'ENMIG

DE LA VERGE

PLAÇA DE SA DRASSANETA

FOSC

DEL RETIR

VISTA ALEGRE

PLAÇA DE SA RIBA

ES MURO

JES PASSADIS

SANT PERE

Sa Torre

PEDRERA

SA LLOVETA

Baluard de Santa Llúcia

SA CARROSSA

Església Sant Pere

GEN BALANSAT

Ajuntament

PLAÇA D'ESPANYA

RESTAURANTS

Bon Profit	13
Comidas Bar San Juan	4
El Bistro	29
El Pirata	11
La Brasa	12
La Plaza	26
La Torreta	20
Macao Café	21
Pasajeros	10
Restaurant Victoria	3
Thai'd Up	24

BARS, CAFÉS & CLUBS

Anfora	28
Bar JJ	23
Bar Red	30
Bar Zuka	22
Base Bar	16
Can Pou Bar	1
Capricho	19
Croissant Show	17
Dôme	25
La Tierra	9
Lola's	27
Madagascar	6
Mao Rooms	5
Montesol	2
Noctámbula	14
Oriental	25
Rock Bar	15
Soap Café	18
Sunset Café	7
Teatro Pereira	8

by the city walls to the south and the sea to the north. Its dilapidated houses constitute both Ibiza's main gypsy district, home to the most marginalized of Spain's population, and also the island's gay village. Sa Penya has an unmistakeably edgy, underground appeal, an identity derived from the crumbling facades of the dark, warren-like alleys and lanes, and the outrageous streetlife, bars and boutiques, all of which create a vibrant and absorbing scene. If you want to explore the *barrio* it's probably best to stick to the area around c/d'Alfons XII and c/de la Verge, as the quieter streets are poorly lit and can be unsafe at night.

Carrer de la Verge

Cutting through the heart of Sa Penya is *the* gay street in Ibiza, Carrer de la Verge (also signposted as c/de la Mare de Déu), lined with dozens of tiny cave-like bars, restaurants and a fetish boutique or two. Despite its inappropriate moniker, the "street of the virgin" is easily the wildest on the island. An ordinary-looking, sleepy lane by day, at night it metamorphoses into a dark, urban alley dedicated to gay hedonism, reverberating to pounding hard house and all-round cacophony. Moving west to east, the street becomes progressively busier, narrower and more raucous, finally becoming no more than a couple of paces wide and crammed with perfectly honed muscle. Up in the balconies drag queens and club dancers preen themselves for the long night ahead, while down below a frenzy of flirtation and bravado fills the air. Just before the rocky cliff that signifies the end of the street, **Sa Torre**, a small stone defensive tower, is a wonderful place to take in night-time views of the lights of Formentera and the Botafoc peninsula.

Carrer d'Alfons XII

During daylight hours Carrer d'Alfons XII is a pleasant but unremarkable corner of Sa Penya, framed by tottering five- and six-storey whitewashed houses and the city walls. Dotted with palm-shaded benches, it's bordered by a small octagonal building, the city's old fish market, which rarely opens these days. By night, however, the plaza-like

▼CLUB PARADE

Dalt Vila's walls

Encircling the entire historic quarter of Dalt Vila, Ibiza Town's monumental Renaissance-era walls are the city's most distinctive structure. Completed in 1585 and still in near-perfect condition, the walls – at almost 2km long, 25m high and up to 5m thick – are some of Europe's best-preserved fortifications, and form a key part of the city's UNESCO World Heritage recognition. The Carthaginians first built walls close to today's castle around the fifth century BC, fortifications that were later extended during the Moorish occupation – remnants from this period survive below the Baluard de Sant Jordi and on c/Sant Josep. Battered by centuries of attacks from pirates, the city's crumbling walls were replaced in the sixteenth century by vast new fortifications, designed by Giovanni Battista Calvi and Jacobo Fratín, that included seven colossal bastions (*baluards*).

street is transformed into one of Ibiza's most flamboyant arenas – the final destination for the summer club parades. At around 1am, after an hour or so of posturing, the podium dancers, promoters and drag queens come together here for a final encore. A surging, sociable throng spills out of some of the most stylish bars on the island to people-watch, blag guest passes and discuss plans for the night's clubbing.

Dalt Vila

Occupying a craggy peak south of the harbour, the ancient settlement of Dalt Vila ("high town") is the oldest part of Ibiza Town and one of its quietest corners. The inhabitants are a disparate mix: the clergy, pockets of Ibizan high society and wealthy foreigners seduced by the superb views and tranquil atmosphere. Alongside the major attractions there are a number of sights to look out for including the walls themselves (see box), and the unadorned whitewashed facade of the fifteenth-century **Església de l'Hospital**, originally a hospital for the poor, but now a low-key cultural centre at the end of c/Sant Josep. **Carrer Major** contains some of the grandest mansions (some bearing family

coats-of-arms) and, close to its western end, a curious chapel, the **Capella de Sant Ciriac**. Little more than a shrine-in-the-wall protected by a metal grille, it is said to be the entrance to a secret tunnel through which the Catalans and Aragonese stormed the Moorish citadel on August 8, 1235 – a special mass is held here to mark the date (see p.172).

Portal de ses Taules

The main entrance into Dalt Vila is the appropriately imposing Portal de ses Taules (Gate of the Inscriptions). The approach alone quickens the pulse: up a mighty stone ramp, across a drawbridge and over a dried-up moat – all part of the defences necessary to keep out sixteenth-century pirates. A stone plaque mounted above the gate bears the coat of arms of Felipe II. Flanking the *portal* are two white marble statues (replicas of a Roman soldier and the goddess Juno). After passing through the gateway you enter the old **Pati d'Armes** (armoury court), a surprisingly graceful, shady arena – the island's very first hippy market was held here in the 1960s. The armoury court leads into graceful **Plaça de Vila**, bordered by elegant old whitewashed mansions, where there are pavement cafés, upmarket restaurants and an assortment of art galleries and boutiques.

▲PORTAL DE SES TAULES

Museu d'Art Contemporani

May–Sept Tues–Fri 10am–1.30pm & 5–8pm, Sat 10am–1.30pm; Oct–April Tues–Fri 10am–1pm & 4–6pm, Sat 10am–1pm. €3. Ibiza's small Museu d'Art Contemporani is housed in a former arsenal; the building was begun in 1727 and later used as a barracks and as the stables of the Infantry Guard. The exhibits are frequently shuffled around, but the work of island-born Tur Costa and the challenging abstract art of Ibiza visitors Will Faber, Hans Hinterreiter and Erwin Broner stand out. Visitors enter the upper floor of the building, the old arms hall, where temporary exhibitions – including graffiti and stencil artists' work – are staged under its lofty beamed roof. The lower floor (the old ammunition store and former stables) comprises two rooms separated by a metre-thick dividing wall. This is where the pick of the museum's collection is displayed, mostly the work of artists with an Ibizan connection of some kind.

Museu Arqueològic d'Eivissa i Formentera

April–Sept Tues–Sat 10am–2pm & 5–7.30pm, Sun 10am–2pm; Oct–March Tues–Sat 10am–1pm & 4–6pm, Sun 10am–2pm. €2.50. The Museu Arqueològic d'Eivissa i Formentera provides an overview of Pitiusan history from prehistoric to Islamic times. It's not wildly exciting, but the exhibits are logically arranged and well presented. The building itself is also of interest, its simple stone facade belying a much bigger interior and its role as the Universitat, Ibiza's seat of government for over 300 years until 1717. There's a fine ribbed vault roof in the museum's entrance hall (which was originally a chapel) that dates from the fourteenth century.

▼MUSEU D'ART CONTEMPORANI

Modest Prehistoric and Phoenician remains are housed in the first two rooms, while the Carthaginian exhibits are also pretty meagre considering Ibiza's importance at that time. There is, however, a carved limestone stela, with an inscription dedicated to the fearsome god Baal, who was

▼ CATHEDRAL

associated with a cult involving the sacrifice of children, plus earthenware images of the fertility goddess Tanit. Aside from the original statues of those mounted by the Portal de ses Taules (see p.57), there's an interesting Roman coin or two with the image of the Carthaginian god Bes on the reverse side, reflecting the fairly harmonious crossover between Punic and Roman times.

Cathedral

Daily 10am–1pm; Sun service 10.30am. Free. Dalt Vila's strategic importance is obvious once you reach the Plaça de la Catedral, affording magnificent views over the port area to the open ocean and Formentera. This summit has been a place of worship for two and a half millennia, and the site for a succession of ceremonial structures: Carthaginian and Roman temples, a Moorish-built mosque and the Gothic Catalan cathedral that stands here today. A former parish church, it was granted cathedral status in 1782 after centuries of petitioning by the Ibizan clergy, and dedicated to

Santa Maria de les Neus (Mary of the Snows) – an odd choice considering that Ibiza only gets a light dusting every ten years or so.

Built mostly in the mid-fourteenth century, the cathedral is a simple rectangular structure supported by buttresses and topped by a mighty bell tower. Its sombre, uncluttered lines are at their most aesthetically pleasing from a distance, especially at night from across the harbour when the structure is floodlit. Whitewashed throughout, the interior is much less attractive. Close to the entrance door there's a plaque dedicated to the Francoists and Catholics massacred in 1936 by Catalan Anarchists. Across from the cathedral is the **Reial Curia**, a late Gothic-style courthouse.

The castle

A rambling strip of buildings constructed in a fractious contest of architectural styles, the castle squats atop the very highest ground in Dalt Vila. Construction began in the eighth century, although modifications were still being made as late as the eighteenth century. During the Spanish Civil War, the castle was the setting for one of the darkest chapters in Ibizan history, when mainland Anarchists, briefly in control of the island, massacred over a hundred Ibizan Nationalist prisoners here before fleeing the island. Left to decay since the mid-twentieth century, the latest plan is to turn the entire complex into a luxury Parador hotel.

For the best perspective of the crumbling facade, head south to the Baluard de Sant Bernat. From here you can make out the sixteenth-century former governor's residence – slab-fronted, dusty pink and with three iron balconies – and rising above this to the left the towers of the Almudaina, the Moorish keep. Smack in the middle of the castle complex is a Moorish fortification, the Tower of Homage, while dropping down in elevation to the left are the wonky-windowed eighteenth-

century infantry barracks.

The southerly views from Sant Bernat are also spectacular, with Formentera clearly visible on the horizon and the sprawling Ibiza resorts of Figueretes and Platja d'en Bossa hugging the coastline just a couple of kilometres away.

Plaça d'Espanya and Sa Carrossa

Directly below the cathedral, Plaça d'Espanya is a narrow, open-ended cobbled square shaded by palm trees. The imposing arcaded building with the domed roof that dominates the plaza was originally built as a Dominican monastery in 1587, before being converted to today's **Ajuntament** (town hall). To the rear of the Ajuntament is one of Ibiza's most handsome churches, the whitewashed sixteenth-century **Església de Sant Pere** (also known as Sant Domingo, open only for services), topped by red-tiled domes and constructed by Genoese master craftsmen. At the eastern end of the plaza (from where there are fine sea views) is a recumbent statue of Guillem de Montgrí, a crusading Catalan baron who helped drive the Moors from Ibiza in 1235. It's a short walk from here along the edge of the walls, to the vast, five-sided **Baluard de Santa Llúcia**, the largest of the seven bastions that define the perimeters of Ibiza Town's walls; rows of cannons are mounted along its battlements.

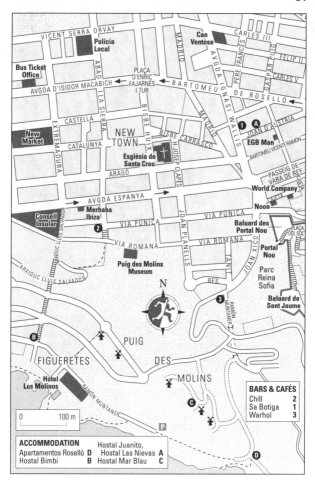

West of here, pretty **Sa Carrossa**, lined with restaurants, plane trees and flowering shrubs, has a statue of a miserable-looking figure: historian and Ibizan author, Isidor Macabich, though he was known for his sardonic sense of humour.

Vara de Rey and around

An imposing and graceful tree-lined boulevard, Vara de Rey, lined with beautiful early twentieth-century buildings, is the hub of modern Ibiza. It's here that you'll find the island's oldest cinema, the Art Deco-style Cine Serra, one of Ibiza's most famous café-bars, the *Montesol* (see p.74) and a collection of fashionable boutiques. Smack in the middle of the avenue is a large stone-and-iron monument dedicated to Ibiza-born General Joachim Vara de Rey, who died in the

▲BUSKERS, PLAÇA DES PARC

Battle of Caney fought between Spain and the USA over Cuba in 1889.

Just a block to the south, the **Plaça des Parc** is an even more inviting place for a coffee or a snack, night or day, with a myriad of café-bars and restaurants grouped around a square shaded by acacias and palms. There's no traffic at all to contend with here, and the small plaza attracts an intriguing mix of stylish Ibizan denizens and plenty of bohemian characters. The bars all have plenty of atmosphere: try *Sunset Café* or *Madagascar* (see p.70).

Puig des Molins

Necropolis: March–Oct Tues–Sat 10am–2pm & 6–8pm, Sun 10am–2pm; Nov–Feb Tues–Sat 9am–3pm, Sun 10am–2pm. Free. Puig des Molins (Hill of the Windmills) was one of the most important Punic burial sites in the Mediterranean. It was chosen by the Phoenicians in the seventh century BC because their burial requirements specified a site free from poisonous creatures – there are no snakes or scorpions on Ibiza. Noblemen were buried on this necropolis in their thousands, their bodies transported here from all over the empire.

Despite its UNESCO World Heritage status, Puig des Molins today is pretty unassuming to look at, appearing little more than a barren rocky park scattered with olive trees. However, the hillside is riddled with over three thousand tombs, and excavations over the years have unearthed some splendid terracotta figurines, amphorae and amulets; most of the finds are gathered in the museum building adjacent to the site, which is unfortunately closed indefinitely. A short trail winds around the site, however, passing Chamber 3 which contains thirteen stone sarcophagi from Punic times. There are also some Punic artefacts at the Museu Arqueològic d'Eivissa i Formentera (see p.58).

New Harbour and Botafoc

Occupying the western and northern sides of Ibiza Town's bay, the New Harbour (or Port

▲BOTAFOC MARINA

road running along its length and a lighthouse defining the final rocky extremity – cava-swigging revellers traditionally congregate here to witness the first sunrise of the New Year. Beyond the lighthouse, a new concrete mole (completed in 2003 to accommodate cruise ships) juts into the harbour waters, offering photographers an arresting perspective of the fortress-like summit of Dalt Vila from across the waves.

Talamanca

Boat from La Marina, May–Oct 9am–1am every 15–30min; 10min. A sweeping sandy bay 2km north of Ibiza Town (a 30min walk via the New Harbour along Passeig de Juan Carlos I), Talamanca beach rarely gets overcrowded, despite its close proximity to the capital. Development has been fairly restrained here, with hotels mainly confined to the northern and southern fringes, and it's not impossible to imagine the paradisiacal pre-tourism environment. A smattering of bars and some good fish restaurants occupy the central part of the shoreline, which is popular with European families – the gently shelving beach is ideal for children.

d'Eivissa) is a recent extension to the city. This area was one half of the capital's vegetable patch, Ses Feixes, until the late 1950s, when the town began to expand to the north. Today, it's a wealthy enclave containing the yacht club, several marinas, luxury apartment blocks, the casino and the clubs *El Divino* and *Pacha* (see p.77 & p.78).

From the *Ocean Drive* hotel, the thin, kilometre-long Botafoc peninsula stretches southeast into the harbour, with a wide

▼TALAMANCA BEACH

Just behind the northern section of the beach, the upmarket suburb of **Can Pep Simó** contains a cluster of striking Modernist villas designed by the Catalan architect Josep Lluís Sert.

s'Estanyol

Best approached from the north side of Talamanca beach, on a signposted route that takes you 1km down a tarmacked road, then 2km down a bumpy dirt track, the idyllic sandy cove of s'Estanyol is one of Ibiza's most isolated bays. There's a small patch of sand and plenty of rocky ledges for sunbathing, as well as one of the island's best *chiringuitos*, the funky *PK s'Estanyol* (May–Oct), selling fresh fish, and paella feasts on Sundays. This *chiringuito* is also occasionally used as an after-party venue.

Jesús

Just northeast of Ibiza Town, along the road to Cala Llonga, Jesús is an overspill of the capital suspended in a suburban no-man's land; it's just urban enough to boast a happening late-night bar, *La Alternativa*

(see p.74), but rural enough to ensure that roosters prevent any chance of a lie-in.

Just off the highway in the centre of the village the whitewashed church, **Nostra Mare de Jesús** (Thurs 10am–noon, plus Sunday Mass), boasts a wonderfully simple Ibizan design dating back to 1466. The church boasts the island's finest altar painting, by Valencians Pere de Cabanes and Rodrigo de Osona. An impressive and expansive work spread over seven main and thirteen smaller panels, with images of Christ, the Virgin Mary and the Apostles, it was deemed of sufficient artistic merit to be spared during the Civil War, when most of the island's ecclesiastical art was destroyed. Opposite the church are *Bon Lloc* (see p.71) and *Croissantería Jesús* (see p.70).

Figueretes

The suburb-cum-resort of Figueretes lies only a fifteen-minute walk southwest of the capital. Although there's a basic seaside appeal here and an attractive palm-lined promenade, the sandy beach, backed by a

▼ EL CORSARIO

dense concentration of unruly apartment blocks, isn't one of the island's finest. Unlike many Ibizan resorts, there's a small resident population, and in winter when the tourists have gone, elderly Ibizans reclaim the streets to stroll, chat and take the sea air.

Undoubtedly one of the most happening places in Ibiza during the 1950s (a bohemian collection of Dutch writers and artists including Jan Gerhard Toonder spent several seasons here) and the focus of the early beatnik scene in the 1960s, there's little evidence today of Figueretes' funky past. Nightlife and eating-out options are limited and the main draw is location – Figueretes makes a convenient and economic base for serious forays into the dynamic night scene just around the bay. Gay visitors have known this for years, and many return annually to the same apartments.

Hotels

El Corsario

c/Ponent 5, Dalt Vila ☎971 301 248, ☎971 391 953, ⊛www .ibiza-hotels.com/CORSARIO. Former pirate's den that's now an atmospheric landmark hotel in the heart of Dalt Vila; Dalí and Picasso allegedly stayed here in the 1950s. The rooms are quite small for the price, but have plenty of character, with beamed roofs and period furniture; some have dramatic harbour views, while the suites (€220–430) have more space including a lounge. The in-house restaurant is overpriced. Prices drop a little in winter. €130–160.

El Hotel

Passeig Marítim, New Harbour ☎971 315 963, ⊛www.elhotelpacha .com. The best hotel in Ibiza Town, owned by *Pacha* (see p.78) and successfully marrying modernist design with Ibiza rustic chic. The huge suite-size rooms really have a wow factor, boasting Phillipe Starck-style furnishings and bathrooms, and though the suites are extremely spacious and boast every luxury imaginable, the rack rates are absurd (€700–1000). Stunning restaurant and an über-hip lounge bar, though the decked pool area is small and not a great place to relax. Breakfast is included. €225–330.

Hostal La Marina

c/Barcelona 7, La Marina ☎971 310 172, ⊛www.ibiza-spotlight.com/ hostal-lamarina/home_i.htm. Historic portside hotel at the heart of the action. There's a choice of accommodation, with stylish, good-value rooms – most have wrought-iron beds, air con and satellite TV – divided between three neighbouring houses, and there's also another cheaper annexe (€52–72) in the New Town. Many rooms in the main *La Marina* building have balconies or terraces, some facing the harbour. €77–100.

Hostal Mar Blau

Puig des Molins ☎971 301 284. May–Oct. Lofty hilltop location, with views over Figueretes beach, yet just a 5min walk from the centre of town. The simply furnished rooms (with lounge areas: €80–100) are a little old-fashioned but spacious, and most come with balconies. Book rooms 3, 4, 211 or 212 for great sea views. There's a sun terrace and breakfast is available (but not included). €50–70.

Hostal Parque

Plaça des Parc 4, New Town ☎971 301 358, ✉hostalparque@hotmail. com. Very central mid-range hotel with tastefully presented, spotless if smallish rooms, all with air con and TV, many with fine views over one of Ibiza Town's prettiest squares. Book well ahead. Single rooms (with shared bath) cost €45–55 and are fair value. €72–100.

Hotel Es Vivé

c/Carles Roman Ferrer 8, Figueretes ☎971 301 902, ⊛www.hotelesvive .com. May–Oct. Chic hotel with contemporary interior design, that's become something of a Balearic HQ for the UK club crowd, and has even spawned its own CD series. Two hip bars (open till 6am), a small pool, and excellent, if pricey food from a modish menu. The rooms are on the small side however, and simply decorated, though all have air con. Beauty treatments and massages are available; breakfast is included. Beware the price rises and four-night minimum stay between Thursdays and Mondays. €125–176.

Hotel Lux Isla

c/Josep Pla 1, Talamanca ☎971 313 469, ⊛www.luxisla.com. Just 75m from Talamanca's beach and 2km from Ibiza Town, this small, attractive hotel has modern comfortable rooms, all with satellit e TV, and most with sea views, while air con is an optional extra at €9 a day. An absolute bargain in winter. €58–95.

La Torre del Canónigo

c/Major 8, Dalt Vila ☎971 303 884, ⊛www.elcanonigo.com. Easter–New Year. Highly atmospheric hotel occupying part of a fourteenth-century defence tower, in a fine location next to the cathedral in Dalt Vila. Offers real historic character, and the suite-sized rooms have either harbour or city views, air con, kitchen facilities, satellite TV, DVD and CD players. Guests have access to a swimming pool close by. The only drawback is the hike uphill from the port area. Suites (€300–480), one with a terrace Jacuzzi, are also available. Prices plummet in winter. €180–210.

▲HOTEL ES VIVÉ

▲LA VENTANA

La Ventana

Sa Carrossa 13, Dalt Vila ☎971 390 857, ⊛www.laventanaibiza.com. Classy converted mansion just inside Dalt Vila's walls that oozes character with hallways full of antique furnishings and Asian fabrics. The twelve rooms are not large, but have every mod con, including air con and four-poster beds; most have great harbour views and some have balconies (€221), as do the two magnificent suites (€387). Excellent restaurant and rooftop terrace. Book well ahead. Rates drop by a third in winter. €156.

Ocean Drive

Marina Botafoc ☎971 318 112, ⊛www.oceandrive.de. Positioned overlooking the Botafoc marina, and close to Talamanca beach, *Pacha* and *El Divino*, this is a stylish address that exudes Miami Art Deco character. Rooms are not large, but are attractive, and all have air con; many have harbour views. Considering there's no pool, summer rates are expensive, though prices drop by half in winter. Decent restaurant. €127–197.

Pensions

Casa de Huéspedes Vara de Rey

Vara de Rey 7, New Town ☎971 301 376 ⊛www.ibiza-spotlight. com/huespedes/index.html. Excellent centrally located hostel with friendly management. The clean attractive rooms (eight singles and three doubles) are simply but artistically furnished with seashell-encrusted mirrors and driftwood wardrobes; all share bathrooms. Streetside rooms can be a little noisy in high season. Rates drop outside peak season. €60–79.

Hostal Bimbi

c/Ramón Muntaner 55, Figueretes ☎971 305 396, ⓕ971 305 396. May–Oct. Backpacker-friendly, family-run *hostal* just a block from Figueretes beach and a ten-minute walk from the heart of Ibiza Town. Nineteen clean, attractive rooms with washbasins and wardrobes, two with private bathroom. €40–45.

Hostal Juanito and Hostal Las Nievas

c/Joan d'Austria 18, New Town ☎971 315 822. These two neighbouring, centrally located *hostals*, popular with young travellers, have clean and tidy budget rooms, some en suite. Both share the same management and prices. Always busy, so book ahead. €38–45.

Sol y Brisa

Avgda Bartomeu Vicente Ramón 15, New Town ☎971 310 818, ℗971 303 032. Cheap, clean and friendly family-run place on a side street close to the port. The twenty rooms are small and share bathrooms, but are good value. €39–45.

Apartments

Apartamentos Roselló

c/Juli Cirer i Vela, Es Soto ☎ & ℗971 302 790. Most of these spacious, comfortable apartments have wonderful sun terraces or large balconies positioned right above the Mediterranean with views to Formentera. All except the singles have a bedroom with twin beds, and a large sunny living area with two more day beds, plus full cooking facilities. The location is very tranquil, yet just a five-minute walk from both Figueretes beach and the heart of Ibiza Town. Very reasonable prices, especially outside high season, and an extremely helpful Ibizan owner. €78–90.

Shops

Boutique Divina

c/Santa Creu, Dalt Vila. With racks and racks of couture for men, women and children, this is one of Ibiza's most renowned "Ad Lib" (loose, flowing white linen) fashion stores. Not cheap.

Can Felix

c/Antoni Palau 1, La Marina. A diverse selection of wonderful traditional and modern fans and costume and beaded shawls at moderate prices.

DJ Beat

Plaça de la Tertulia, La Marina. One of Ibiza's premier record stores. Racks of dance vinyl, and some mixed electronica and lounge CDs too.

▼DJ BEAT

▲CROISSANT SHOW

EGB Man

c/Vincent Cuervo 11, New Town. Modish menswear boutique, geared towards a gay clientele, with a good range of flamboyant shirts, fitted T-shirts and some underwear.

El Secreto de Baltasar

Comte Roselló 6, La Marina. Ibiza's most beautiful shoe store, with a great selection of moderately priced men's and women's leather footwear, plus brands including No Name, DKNY and Bunker.

Envy

c/G. de Montgrí 22, La Marina. Very affordable boutique offering groovy, highly individualistic girly clubwear and accessories.

Merhaba Ibiza

Avgda d'Espanya 43, New Town. Warehouse-style store, with racks of very inexpensive women's boho garb, beaded sandals and beach wear.

Natural

Plaça des Parc, New Town. Fabrics, cushion covers, sofa throws and jewellery, all with an ethnic flavour.

Noon

Caietà Soler 9, New Town. Stunning bookshop-cum-café with good stock of design, fashion, film and music titles. There's Internet access too.

Sing Sing

c/de sa Creu 9, La Marina. Cheap, hip girls' gear, with lots of bold prints and ruffled tops – it helps if you're a size 8.

World Company

c/Caietà, New Town. Terrific range of mainly Italian, seriously stylish sunglasses. Good value, with prices from around €20 to over €100.

Cafés

Chill

Via Púnica 49, New Town. Daily 10am–midnight. Friendly Internet café, and a popular hangout in its own right, with funky decor and a good noticeboard. Healthy food and drink: fruit salads, pitta bread sandwiches and pastries, as well as huge frothy coffees, herbal teas, fresh juices, shakes, beers, wine and spirits.

Croissant Show

Plaça de sa Constitució, La Marina. Daily: April–June & Oct 6am–2am; July–Sept open 24hr. Located right by the main gateway to Dalt Vila this place bakes some of the finest patisserie in town – though service can be defiantly negligent at times. One of La Marina's most famous cafés, it's often lively around dawn, when the party people gather to perform a postmortem on the night's action.

Croissantería Jesús

Ctra Cala Llonga, Jesús. Wed–Sun 7am–3pm. One of the finest places for breakfast in Ibiza; pick and mix from flaky butter-rich croissants, muesli, fresh juices, wholemeal toast, eggs and ham, or opt for one of the set deals. There's a pavement terrace and a cheery interior decorated with old Martini signs.

Madagascar

Plaça des Parc, New Town. Daily: May–Sept 9am–2am; Oct–April 9am–midnight. Perhaps the pick of the cafés on pretty Plaça des Parc, *Madagascar* is stylish rather than self-consciously chic, and attracts a disparate clientele. Great juices (try the mixed carrot and fresh orange) and a limited food menu, plus very fine mocha-tinged *café con leche*.

Sa Botiga

Avgda d'Ignaci Wallis 14, New Town. Daily noon–midnight. With rattan chairs, monochrome photographs, sandstone walls and a palm-shaded rear patio this is one of Ibiza Town's most elegant cafés. Tempting tapas, a well-priced *menú del día*, draught Guinness and some decent wines.

Sunset Café

Plaça des Parc, New Town. Daily 9am–2am. Stylish bar-café that attracts a loyal clientele, including a regular bunch of boho characters from the north of the island. Ideal place for a late breakfast of fresh juice and a *tostada*. The striking decor combines animal prints, velvet and neo-industrial fixtures; the music evolves from chilled daytime tunes to live DJ sets.

Restaurants

Bar Flotante

Talamanca beach ☎971 190 466. Daily 11am–11pm. At the southern end of Talamanca beach, this cheap, informal and popular café-restaurant has a large plot right by the waves – you can almost dangle your feet in the sea while you eat. Huge portions, with good fish and seafood – try the *sardinas a la plancha*. Children are very welcome and it's also a great place for a humble *bocadillo* and a glass of wine.

▼MADAGASCAR

▲ RESTAURANTS ON SA CARROSSA

Bon Lloc

Ctra Cala Llonga, Jesús. Daily 7am–midnight. Unpretentious, inexpensive village bar-restaurant that's crammed in the early mornings with Ibizan workers downing brandy and *café solo*, and puffing Ducados. Later on, it's ideal for tapas or a set meal (€7.50) in the large interior or streetside terrace.

Bon Profit

Plaça des Parc 5, New Town. Mon–Sat 1–3.30pm & 7.30–10.30pm. No reservations. Terrific canteen-style dining room, with stylish decor and shared tables. Bargain-priced menu of Spanish meat, fish and vegetable dishes – try the lamb shank casserole. It's always very popular, with queues in summer.

Comidas Bar San Juan

c/G. de Montgri 8, La Marina. Daily 1–3.30pm & 8–11.30pm. No reservations. Venerable restaurant that's been run by the same hospitable family for generations, with two tiny, wood-panelled rooms and inexpensive (€4–9) flavoursome Spanish and Ibizan dishes. You

may be asked to share a table, particularly in high season.

El Bistro

Sa Carrossa 15, Dalt Vila ☏971 393 203, ⊛www.elbistrorestaurante. com. Easter–Oct daily 7.30pm–1am. One of Dalt Vila's most welcoming restaurants, with fine Mediterranean food served on the pavement terrace or in the intimate dining room. It's slightly cheaper than most places in Dalt Vila, and good value given the location. The grilled meats are good, including pork fillet with peppercorns, while foie gras is a house speciality and there are plenty of salad starters. Wines are well priced too.

El Parador

c/Portinatx 2, Can Escandell ☏971 300 536. Terrific inexpensive and informal Argentinian-style restaurant located on the corner of the busy Avgda de Sant Josep road about 1km west of Ibiza Town. It's all about meat, as racks of beef sizzle and spit on the vast *parrilla* (barbecue), though all dishes come with chips and salad. Grab a table in the tiled interior or sit outside next to the highway.

El Pirata

c/Garijo 10B, La Marina ☎971 192 630. May–Sept 8pm–2am. Authentic, friendly Italian-owned pizzeria, in the heart of the port area, where you can eat terrific thin-crust pizza on a harbourfront pavement terrace.

Gusto

Passeig Juan Carlos 1, New Harbour ☎971 192 645. April–Oct Mon–Sat 7.30pm–1am. Very stylish restaurant, on the north side of Ibiza Town's harbour, set up by the English-Argentinian team that ran the renowned *Kasbah* in Sant Antoni for years. The cooking here is consistently excellent, arguably the best in Ibiza, with a contemporary, metropolitan-style line-up of creatively presented meat and fish dishes (including superb herb-crusted tuna steak at €15.50) and to-die-for desserts (€5).

La Brasa

c/Pere Sala 3, La Marina ☎971 301 202. Noon–4pm & 7.30pm–12.30am. This restaurant boasts the port area's loveliest garden terrace that's perfect for summer dining, and there's also an attractive interior (where a log fire burns in winter). The moderately expensive Mediterranean menu is meat- and fish-based, with daily specials using seasonal ingredients.

La Plaza

Plaça de Vila 18, Dalt Vila ☎971 307 617. May–Oct daily 1–4pm & 7.30pm–midnight. Superbly sited just inside the main Dalt Vila gateway this classic Mediterranean restaurant has a great pavement terrace and tiled dining room. There's an excellent selection of meat and fish dishes (from €14) and reasonably priced pasta (from €8.50).

La Torreta

Plaça de Vila, Dalt Vila ☎971 300 411. May–Sept daily 1–3.30pm & 7pm–1am. Of the many fine places to eat in Dalt Vila's Plaça de Vila, *La Torreta* offers some of the best cuisine, particular seafood and desserts, though expect to pay around €50 a head. There's an extensive pavement terrace, or for a really memorable setting, book the inside room that occupies one of the Dalt Vila's original bastions.

Macao Café

Plaça de sa Riba, Sa Penya ☎971 314 707, ✇www.macaocafe.com. Daily: May–Oct 1–4pm & 7.30pm–1am; Nov–April 7.30–11.30pm. Enjoyable, relaxed Italian restaurant at the eastern end of the harbour, with an extensive portside terrace. The creatively assembled and moderately priced menu includes watercress and goats' cheese salad, grilled meat dishes and particularly good fresh pasta – try the linguine with zucchini and shrimps.

Pasajeros

1st Floor, c/Vicent Soler, La Marina (no phone). May–Sept daily 7.30pm–12.30am. Cramped, cheap first-floor canteen-like diner that despite appearances delivers some of the tastiest, best-value food in town: good salads, filling meat dishes (try the chicken with roquefort), plenty of vegetarian options (including delicious creamed spinach) and inexpensive wines. Many of Ibiza's hardcore club crowd get their sustenance here so it's a good place to find out what's going on.

▲ BASE BAR

Restaurante Soleado

Passeig de ses Pitiuses, Figueretes
☏971 394 811. May–Oct daily
1–3.30pm & 7.30–midnight. The
finest restaurant in Figueretes,
with a delightful seafront terrace
positioned just above the sea,
with views across to Formentera.
There's an extensive Provençal-
based menu with good fish and
seafood and meat mains. Around
€35–40 per person.

Restaurant Victoria

c/Riambau 1, La Marina ☏971 310
622. May–Oct 1–3.30pm & 9–11pm;
Nov–April 1–3.30pm & 7.30–10.30pm.
Charming, old-fashioned
Spanish *comedor* (canteen),
with simple furnishings and a
welcoming ambience. It serves
very inexpensive but well-
prepared Spanish and Ibizan
meat and fish dishes, and plenty
of robust wines.

Thai'd Up

c/de la Verge 78, Sa Penya ☏971 191
668. May–Sept daily 8.30pm–midnight.
Great Thai grub, served alfresco
at the very eastern end of Sa
Penya, or in a tiny inside dining
area. Friendly, attentive service;
the curries, *pad thai* noodles

and spicy soups are fresh and
authentic.

Bars

Bar Zuka

c/de la Verge 75, Sa Penya. April–Oct
daily 9pm–4am. One of Ibiza
Town's most stylish and
enjoyable bars, with antique
mirrors, imposing artwork
and an "eagle's nest" balcony
table with harbour views. Less
frenetic than many bars in the
port zone, and a great place to
converse and meet people. The
music has a real Balearic flavour,
and the ever-attentive English
owner is full of entertaining
anecdotes about the island.

Base Bar

c/Garijo 15–16, La Marina ⊛www.
basebaribiza.com. May–Oct daily
9pm–3.30am. Portside HQ for
a hedonistic crowd of (mainly
British) clubbers, dance
industry folk and well-seasoned
scenesters; there's a raucous
buzz about this bar all summer
long. Run by a veteran party-
hard crew, the *Base Bar* has also
spawned several CDs.

Can Pou Bar

c/Lluís Tur i Palau 19, La Marina.
Daily: May–Oct noon–2am; Nov–April
11am–1am. Enjoys a prime
position by the harbourside and
has a quirky, disparate clientele
of Ibizan artists, intellectuals and
the odd drunk. One of the few
bars open in this area outside
summer. Music is a mere
distraction as island politics are
discussed and black tobacco
puffed in the wood-panelled
interior. Tasty *bocadillos* are
available.

Grial

Avgda 8 de d'Agost 11. June–Sept
daily 8pm–4am; Oct–May Tues–Sun
9.30pm–4am. Popular locals'
hangout, with live DJs most
nights spinning everything from
electro to hip hop. With *Pacha*
almost next door, it's a key
meeting point for clubbers, and
a good place to visit in winter,
when virtually all the port bars
are closed.

▼CAN POU BAR

La Alternativa

c/de la Gaviota, Jesús. Daily 8pm–5am.
Probably the closest thing to a
pub on the whole island, with
four rooms, a pool table and
dartboard – but alas, no draught
ales. After midnight, DJs spin
house, funk and rock to a mixed
crowd of clubbers, bikers and
island headcases.

La Tierra

Passatge Trinitat 4, off c/Barcelona,
La Marina. Daily 9pm–3am. Steeped
in hippy folklore this was the
scene of major "happenings" in
the 1960s. There's less patchouli
oil around these days, but the
ambience remains vibrant,
carried by an eclectic mix of
hard-drinking Ibizans. Musically,
things are kept funky, and there
are regular live DJ sets.

Mao Rooms

c/Emili Pou 6, La Marina. May–Oct
daily 10pm–3.30am; Nov–April Thurs–
Sun only. Hip, happening bar,
owned by London's *Chinawhite*,
with opium den-inspired decor
of velvet curtains and alcoves
strewn with luxuriant cushions
and a connected crowd of
fashionista regulars. Hosts well-
attended parties by the likes of
Sancho Panza.

Montesol

Vara de Rey, New Town. Daily
8am–midnight. One of Ibiza
high society's main destinations,
and popular with the mature,
perma-tanned, Gucci-toting
crowd. Punctilious service from
immaculately attired waiters, and
prices are far from outrageous
considering the location and
reputation.

Noctámbula

c/des Passadís 18, Sa Penya. May–Oct
daily 9pm–3am. Enjoyable, street-
chic Italian-owned place with an

▲MONTESOL

outdoor terrace and quirky bar area that has plenty of nooks and crannies. DJs mix hard house to a party crowd, and there's a little chillout zone upstairs.

Rock Bar

c/Garijo 14, La Marina. May–Oct daily 9pm–3am. Ibizan institution, next to the *Base Bar*, run by some of the best-known faces in the local scene, and drawing a slightly older, more international crowd than its neighbour. The *Rock Bar* has a stylish cream interior, DJ decks and a capacious terrace which is one of Ibiza's most celebrated summer hangouts.

Teatro Pereira

c/Comte Roselló. Daily 9am–5am. Set in what was the foyer of a fine nineteenth-century theatre, this is Ibiza Town's premier live music venue by night. Jazz bands, mainly playing covers, attract a sociable middle-aged crowd; entrance is free, but drinks are expensive. By day, it's a stylish café, with good creamy coffee, juices and *bocadillos*.

Warhol

c/Ramón Muntaner 145, New Town. Daily 9.30pm–3.30am. Über-chic modernist bar, with cutting-edge minimalist design, drawing a lively local crowd. The glass walls of the bar area look in on a triangular Zen-style garden; DJs spin house and progressive mixes, and there's a good cocktail list.

Gay bars

Bar JJ

c/de la Verge 79, Sa Penya. April to mid-Oct daily 9.30pm–3am. *Bar JJ* has excellent connections to the club scene, and is a good place to score free passes for a night out. The attractive interior has great harbour views, and it's popular with a French and Spanish crowd.

Bar Red

Sa Carrossa 4, Dalt Vila. Daily 9pm–4am. Facing Dalt Vila's walls, this British-owned place is one of the most welcoming and relaxed gay bars in town and is open all year. There's a great pavement terrace for summer quaffing and the owners are full of helpful tips about the island.

▲C/DE LA VERGE

Capricho

c/de la Verge 42, Sa Penya. Easter–Nov daily 9pm–3am. Probably the most happening bar on gay Ibiza's main drag, the perennially popular *Capricho* has a classy interior, beautiful bar boys and perhaps the most gregarious street terrace in town. Draws a youthful German, Dutch and British crowd.

Dôme

c/d'Alfons XII 5, Sa Penya. May–Oct daily 10pm–3am. Gay Ibiza at its most gorgeous: stunning bar staff, horrifically expensive drinks, and perhaps the best location, too, in the plaza-like environs of c/d'Alfons XII. As the final destination of most of the club parades, the atmosphere on the terrace outside reaches fever pitch by 1am during the summer, when it's filled with a riotous assemblage of hipsters, wannabes and drag queens.

Monroe's

c/Ramón Muntaner 33, Figueretes. May–Oct daily 10am–3am. Run by a larger-than-life British lesbian couple, and featured in the nauseous *Ibiza Uncovered* TV series, this temple of kitsch to Hollywood's celluloid goddess has Marilyn memorabilia on every wall. One of the most popular bars in Figueretes, it draws a mixed gay and family crowd, with regular cabaret shows. All rather tacky and passé, but try telling the regulars that.

Oriental

c/d'Alfons XII 3, Sa Penya. Daily 10pm–4am. *Oriental* is one of the hottest bars on the Ibiza gay scene, with resident DJs and strong ties with Amnesia (see p.124), which guarantees the terrace is packed on La Troya club nights. Also open throughout the winter.

Soap Café

c/Manuel Sora 4, La Marina. May–Oct daily 10am–10pm. Just behind the *Croissant Show* (see p.69), *Soap* provides quicker and more friendly service than its more famous neighbour, plus a well-stocked bar and the best crêpes on the island.

▼DÔME

▲ EL DIVINO

Clubs

Anfora

c/Sant Carles 7, Dalt Vila ⊛www.
anfora-disco.com. April–Oct plus Easter
and New Year. €8 until 2am; €12
after. Ibiza's only gay club venue,
Anfora is set inside a natural
cave in the heart of Dalt Vila. It
attracts an international, mixed-
age crowd, with wrinkly drag
queens, the leather posse and
hip young urban boys socializing
freely. Musically, the sounds tend
to reflect the disparate nature
and ages of the regulars, with
resident DJs mixing driving
house with camp anthems. The
club's tiny backstreet Dalt Vila
doorway is deceptive, as inside
there's a large gingham-tiled
dancefloor, a central bar and a
stage (usually used for drag acts).
Upstairs, you'll find a sociable
bar area, and a darkroom which
screens hardcore movies. Door
tax is very reasonable by Ibizan
club standards.

El Divino

New Harbour ⊛www.eldivino-ibiza.com.
Easter–Oct and some winter weekends.
Free shuttle boat from Passeig Marítim
(midnight–3.30am; every 15min). €30–
45. Mustard-coloured, temple-like

El Divino vies with *Pacha* as
the ultimate destination for the
seriously solvent; holding up to
1000 punters it has a stained-
glass lobby, opulent restaurant
and VIP lounge. Jutting into the
Ibiza Town harbour, with water
on three sides, it boasts the most
enviable location of any club on
the island, its arched windows
revealing a panoramic view of the
floodlit old town beyond the port.

Not especially musically
influential (concentrating mainly
on vocal house sounds), it has
traditionally attracted a relaxed,
cosmopolitan crowd who are
slightly more restrained than the
pilled-up punters elsewhere. The
most successful nights in recent
years have included *Hed Kandi*,
Defected and *Miss Moneypenny's*.
Expect a glam, label-conscious
crowd, and fairly reasonable (for
Ibiza) drink prices.

Lola's

c/d'Alfons XII 10, Sa Penya. May–Sept
& some weekends in winter. This
small, intimate club, with a great
location tight against the walls
of Dalt Vila, was a happening
venue in the 1970s. It reopened
in 2004 with Carl Cox playing
the launch night, but after this
initial flurry, the venue fell

off the party radar somewhat. *Lola's* potential, however, is undeniable, with many of Ibiza Town's in crowd crying out for a smaller, more intimate club venue. There's a compact but stylish interior, fully loaded with a decent sound system, and a great adjacent outdoor terrace for socializing. Free or moderate entrance prices, depending on the night.

Pacha

Avgda 8 d'Agost ⊛ www.pacha.es. Easter–Oct, weekends in winter. The one Ibizan club to open all year round, the 3000-capacity *Pacha* is the classiest venue on the island, with faultless decor, professional staff, and the best dancers in Ibiza. More than seventy *Pacha* clubs have established a worldwide identity for their chic, Balearic brand of clubbing. The decidedly international clientele embraces all ages, from young Ibizans to still-swinging playboys, wide-eyed tourists and fifty-year-old salsa fans. Over the years, the most successful nights, including Erick Morillo's Subliminal and Renaissance, have concentrated on uplifting, vocal-rich house music rather than slamming techno or trance – music that suits the crowd.

Pacha opened in 1973 in a farmhouse on the edge of the capital; the whitewashed exterior of the old *finca*, framed by floodlit palm trees, still creates a real sense of occasion. Inside, the beautiful main room has a sunken dancefloor surrounded by tiers; you can also dine in a seriously stylish sushi bar. There's a salsa room, *Pachacha*, a Funky Room, *El Cielo*, and a dark Global Room where you'll find more diverse experimental beats, and R&B and hip-hop on occasions. The elegant terrace, spread over several layers, is a wonderfully sociable, open-air affair, with vistas of the city skyline.

The east

Ibiza's indented eastern coastline is dotted with family-oriented resorts and sheltered coves. Many of the most spectacular sandy beaches, such as Cala Llonga and Cala de Sant Vicent, were developed decades ago into bucket-and-spade holiday enclaves, but plenty of undeveloped bays remain, such as Cala Mastella, the cliff-backed cove of Cala Boix and the kilometre-long unspoilt sands of Aigües Blanques – the place to bare all in the north of the island. Santa Eulària des Riu, the region's municipal capital, is a pleasant but unremarkable town that acts as a focus for the east coast's resorts and has a friendly, familial appeal as well as a lively restaurant strip and a marina. Further north lie pretty Sant Carles and the hamlet of Sant Vicent, surrounded by some of Ibiza's most spectacular scenery: forested hillsides, sweeping valleys, and rugged coves.

Cala Llonga

Buses #15 & #41 from Santa Eulària, May–Oct Mon–Sat 19 daily, Sun 10 daily; 10min. Boats from Santa Eulària, June–Sept 9 daily; 15 min. Heading north from Ibiza Town, the first of the *calas* on the east coast is the small family resort of Cala Llonga. Set in a spectacular inlet below soaring wooded cliffs, the 300-metre-wide bay has fine, gently shelving sand and usually calm, translucent water. The scene is slightly spoilt, however, by the lumpish apartment blocks insensitively built on the northern cliffs. There are full beachside facilities including sunbeds, umbrellas and pedalos, and a tourist information kiosk

▼SOL DEN SERRA

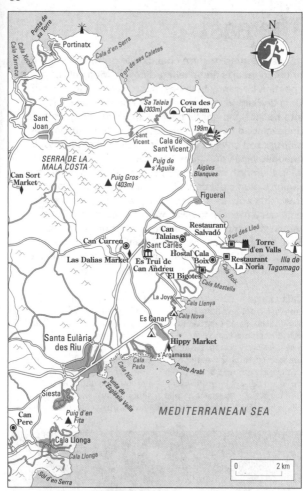

(May–Oct Mon–Sat 10am–2pm). As in many Ibizan resorts, the cuisine on offer here is uninspiring, with little variety.

Sòl d'en Serra

Just 800m south of Cala Llonga, down a bumpy dirt track, Sòl d'en Serra is a slender,

Transport

Getting around the east on **public transport** is fairly easy. Santa Eulària is served by a frequent **bus** from Ibiza Town and also well connected to the area's resorts and villages by regular bus and **boat** services (indicated in the text). However, to get to the more remote beaches, you'll have to arrange your own transport – or take taxis.

Arrival and information

Santa Eulària's **bus** stops (there's no station) are on Avgda Dr Ricardo Curtoys, a block west of the beach. **Boats** leave from a dock on the west side of Port Esportiu. Between June and September they serve Formentera (2 daily day-trips, 1hr 15min one way), Ibiza Town (7 daily, 40min) and beaches to the north and south. There's a **tourist information** kiosk (May–Oct Mon–Fri 9am–1pm & 4–7pm, Sat 9am–1pm; ☎971 330 728) on Passeig de s'Alamera.

undeveloped 500-metre-long pebble beach backed by high golden cliffs. The shore is quite exposed here, and the sea can get choppy on windy days – perfect for an invigorating dip if you're a strong swimmer, but not ideal for small children. The beach never gets busy, even in high season; between October and May, you're almost guaranteed to have it to yourself. Reasonable meals and snacks are served in the *Sòl d'en Serra* restaurant overlooking the waves, which also has a terrace with sunbeds.

Santa Eulària des Riu

Bus from Ibiza Town, May–Sept Mon–Sat every 30min, Sun hourly; Oct–April Mon–Sat hourly, Sun 8 daily; 25min. Boat from Ibiza Town, May–Oct 7 daily; 30min. In an island of excess, Santa Eulària des Riu, Ibiza's third largest town, is remarkable for its ordinariness. Pleasant and provincial, the town lies on the eastern bank of the only river in the Balearics. Its best aspect, however, is its shoreline; the two town **beaches** are clean and tidy, with softly sloping sands that are ideal for children, while the marina, **Port Esportiu**, is a popular place for a pricey drink or meal, although menus tend to be uninspiring. The graceful **Ajuntament** (Town Hall), built in 1795 and sporting a stout-arched colonnade flanked by two simple municipal coats-of-arms, dominates the north side of Plaça d'Espanya. Just below, **Passeig de s'Alamera** is easily Santa Eulària's most attractive thoroughfare, with a shady, tree-lined pedestrianized centre. In summer evenings dozens of market stalls here add a splash of colour, selling jewellery, sarongs and tie-dye garb. There's a good selection of moderately priced restaurants on c/Sant Vicent. Nightlife, however, is pretty tame; most locals and visitors content themselves with a drink in one of the bars along the palm-lined promenade.

▼PASSEIG DE S'ALAMERA, SANTA EULÀRIA

Museu Etnològic d'Eivissa i Formentera

Daily: May–Oct 10am–1pm & 5–8pm; Nov–April 10am–1pm

& 4–5.30pm; €2.40. Halfway up Puig de Missa, the Museu Etnològic d'Eivissa i Formentera has displays based on Pitiusan rural traditions. The main draw here is the museum building itself, a classic example of the traditional flat-roofed Ibizan *casament* house. You enter via the outdoor terrace (*porxet*), while the cool, beamed *porxo* (long room) that now houses the ticket office would have been the heart of the household for most of the year, where corn was husked, tools sharpened and *festeig* (courting rituals) held. Most of the exhibits here are either carpentry tools or musical instruments, such as oleander flutes (*flautas*) and *tambor* drums made from pine and rabbit skin.

All the other rooms lead off the *porxo*. Room 4 houses nineteenth- and early twentieth-century women's clothing.

Downstairs, room 5 is a damp natural cave, perfect for wine storage, where a grape press, vat, cask and decanter are on display. The kitchen (room 6) is dominated by a massive hearth and chimney hood while room 8 has a huge old olive oil press. Up another flight of stairs from the *porxo*, room 9 has fishing spears and a framed privateer's licence, the legal certificate granted to Ibizan corsairs by the Crown, authorizing them to attack pirate vessels.

Església de Puig de Missa

May–Sept daily 9am–9pm. Puig de Missa's 52-metre summit is dominated by the sculpted lines of Santa Eulària's very fine fortress-church, Església de Puig de Missa, a white rectangular building constructed – after pirates destroyed the original chapel

– by the Italian architect Calvi, who was also responsible for the walls of Dalt Vila (see p.57). Dating from 1568, the church has a semicircular tower built into its eastern flank that formed part of Ibiza's coastal defences.

▲ESGLÉSIA DE PUIG DE MISSA

Around 1700, the church's best feature was added: a magnificent and wonderfully cool porch with eight arches and mighty pillars supporting a precarious-looking beamed roof. The church interior is whitewashed throughout, with little decoration apart from a series of images of a suffering Christ and a huge, typically gaudy, *churrigueresque*-style seventeenth-century altar – the original interior was torched in the Spanish Civil War. Below the church, just to the south, the cemetery is worth a quick look, thick with verdant foliage and spilling down the hill over several different levels. Amongst the predominantly Catholic monuments, one tombstone displays a Star of David, in honour of a member of the tiny Jewish community that has been established in Ibiza since Carthaginian times.

Coastal walk to Punta Arabí

From the seafront promenade in Santa Eulària, an attractive, easy-to-follow coastal path follows the shoreline northeast to the modern resort of Es Canar. It's a six-kilometre, two-hour walk, with plenty of opportunities for a swim along the way. Head east along the promenade and after about fifteen minutes you'll reach the rocky promontory of **Punta de s'Església Vella**. The path loops around the bulky, landmark *Hotel Los Soros*, and passes above quiet **Cala Niu Blau**, or "Blue Nest Cove", where there's a 100-metre arc of fine, sunbed-strewn sand and a simple fish restaurant.

Continuing along the coast path, past a cluster of pricey-looking villas, you'll arrive at **Cala Pada** in about twenty minutes; the 200m of fine, pale sand and shallow water here are popular with families, and there are three café-restaurants. It's also a surprisingly well-connected beach, with hourly **boats** to Santa Eulària and Ibiza Town during the summer, when boat operators also offer excursions to Formentera.

Some 500m beyond Cala Pada, the path skirts **s'Argamassa**, a compact, fairly upmarket family resort where a scattering of large modern three- and four-star hotels loom over the shoreline. From here the path heads inland, bypassing the wooded promontory of **Punta Arabí**, which juts into the Mediterranean opposite two tiny rocky islets. It's then a ten-minute stroll into Es Canar, passing the *Club Arabí* resort, where Ibiza's biggest hippy market (see p.84) is held.

Es Canar

Bus #18 from Santa Eulària, May–Oct Mon–Sat 26 daily, Sun 15 daily; Nov–April Mon–Sat 5 daily, Sun 2 daily; 15min. Boats from Santa Eulària, June–Sept 9 daily; 20min; or Ibiza Town 7 daily; 55min. Es Canar, a compact resort of four- and five-storey hotel blocks, lies 5km across the well-watered plain northeast of Santa Eulària. The inviting Blue Flag beach, with an arc of fine sand, is Es Canar's main attraction, with safe swimming in its sheltered waters. Unfortunately, the accompanying tourist facilities – a strip of British and Irish pubs, souvenir shops and fast-food joints – present a much less pleasant picture, though the special menus and happy hours keep things economical at least.

Es Canar is generally a family-oriented place, where children are well catered for and nights revolve around "Miss and Mr Es Canar" competitions and quiz shows. However, it's the vast weekly **hippy market** (May–Oct Wed only 10am–6pm), held just south of the centre in the grounds of the *Club Arabí* resort, that draws most people to this part of the coast, when traffic chokes the area. There's little original stuff at the market, and most of the stalls sell similar overpriced tat and disposable-quality jewellery.

▼HIPPY MARKET, ES CANAR

▲CALA NOVA

Cala Nova

A kilometre north of Es Canar around the rocky coastline, the wide sandy bay of Cala Nova is one of Ibiza's most exposed beaches, with invigorating, churning waves at most times of year, but especially when there's a northerly wind blowing. The sands never get too crowded here however, and there are sunbeds and umbrellas for rent, and a small snack bar (May–Oct).

Sant Carles

Bus #16 or #23 from Santa Eulària, May–Sept Mon–Sat 4 daily, Sun 1 daily; 15min. Of all Ibiza's villages, the pretty, whitewashed settlement of Sant Carles, 7km northeast of Santa Eulària, is probably the most steeped in hippy history. Bohemian travellers started arriving in the 1960s, attracted by vacant farmhouses in the surrounding unspoilt countryside; the village, and specifically *Anita's* bar, became the focus of a lively scene. *Anita's* remains open (see p.90), though these days *Las Dalias* bar (see p.92), nearby, is much more of a boho hangout – it hosts a Saturday market that's well worth a visit for the stalls of ethnic oddities sold by a merry bunch of tie-dye traders and chaiwallahs.

The village **church** is a fine eighteenth-century construction, with a broad, arcaded entrance porch and a simple white interior with a single nave and a side chapel. In 1936, during the Spanish Civil War, the Nationalist priest and his father were both hung from the carob tree that still stands outside the church, after clashes with a group of Republicans.

Es Trui de Can Andreu

May–Sept Mon–Fri 3.30–4.30pm, Sat 11.30am–1.30pm & 3.30–4.30pm; open sporadically in winter, call ☎971 335 261 to check. €3.50. On the outskirts of Sant Carles, 250m south of the church,

the seventeenth-century Es Trui de Can Andreu is a fine example of a traditional Ibizan farmhouse, or *casament*. The whitewashed cubist structure displays all the renowned design features of Ibiza style, so feted by modernist architects. Tiny windows punctuate the house's exterior in seemingly haphazard places, while all the rooms have a certain organic character, with bowed sabina pine-timbered roofs contrasting superbly with chalk-white, metre-thick walls. The prefix "*es trui*" refers to Can Andreu's colossal olive press, the house's most unusual feature, which is kept in the smoke-blackened kitchen. Several other rooms exhibit various Ibizan cultural curios: musical instruments, farming tools including threshers and ploughs, basketry and *espardenyas* sandals. You'll be escorted around the building by a member of the Andreu Torres family, the owners of the house; they no longer live here, but remain proud of their ancestral home and are keen to point out its unusual features. All visitors are offered a glass of local Hierbas liqueur and you can also buy Ibizan wine here.

▼ES TRUI DE CAN ANDREU

▲CALA BOIX

Cala Llenya

Bus #16 from Santa Eulària, May–Oct Mon–Fri 3 daily, Sat 2 daily; 25min. Southeast of Sant Carles, a signposted road weaves 4km downhill through small terraced fields of olive and carob trees before reaching Cala Llenya, a two-hundred-metre wide bite-shaped sandy bay lying between low sandstone cliffs scattered with white-painted villas. The sea can get choppy here and, perhaps because of this, the fine sands never get too crowded – you should have no problem finding a sunbed or umbrella for the day, and there's also a friendly beachside café (May–Oct) for snacks and drinks.

Cala Mastella

Heading north along the coast, the next beach is Cala Mastella, some 3km from Cala Llenya; the route descends to the shore via an idyllic terraced valley. Barely forty metres wide, the sandy beach is lovely, set at the back of a deep coastal inlet with pine trees almost touching the sheltered, emerald waters. It's an exceptionally inviting place for a swim, although watch out

for sea urchins, some of which are fairly close to the shore. A tiny kiosk (May–Sept) rents out sunbeds and sells drinks (including delicious home-made *limonada*), but for a fine seafood lunch walk 50m around the north side of the bay to the *El Bigotes* restaurant (see p.91).

Cala Boix

North of Cala Mastella, a wonderfully scenic coastal road meanders for 1km or so through pine forest, affording panoramic views over the Mediterranean below, before reaching Cala Boix, set below high, crumbling cliffs. It's a beautiful sliver of a beach, with coarse darkish sand and pebbles. Three simple restaurants line the headland high above the shore – *La Noria* commands the best views (see p.91).

Pou des Lleó

Inland of Cala Boix, a lone country road cuts northwest for 1km or so, past large terraced fields separated by honey-coloured dry-stone walls, until you come to a signposted junction for the diminutive bay of Pou des Lleó. A tiny, pebble-and-sand-strewn horseshoe-shaped inlet, surrounded by low-lying, rust-red cliffs and lined with fishing huts, the only facilities here are a tiny snack bar (May–Oct 11am–sunset) serving delicious grilled fish and cold beers, and the decent *Restaurant Salvadó* (see p.91).

Torre d'en Valls

A further kilometre east towards the coast from Pou des Lleó is a seventeenth-century defence tower, Torre d'en Valls, set atop one of the few outcrops of lava rock in Ibiza. The tower is in fine condition and has metal rungs ascending its exterior wall; its door is kept locked however. There are panoramic views over the ocean from here, towards the humpbacked island of Tagomago.

Figueral

Bus #23 from Santa Eulària, June–Sept 3 daily; May & Oct Mon–Fri 3 daily, Sat 1 daily; 25min. Continuing northeast the next resort is Figueral, a small, fairly prosperous but slightly bland place, popular with French and German families. It hosts a clump of hotels, a mediocre restaurant or two and souvenir shops offering postcards and lilos. The narrow, two-hundred-metre stretch of exposed sands is swept clean by churning waves, but swimming conditions can get a little rough when the prevailing northeasterly blows.

Aigües Blanques

Bus #23 from Santa Eulària, June–Sept 3 daily; May & Oct Mon–Fri 3 daily, Sat 1 daily; 30min. The naturist beach of Aigües Blanques, or "White Waters", is separated from Figueral's slender sands

by a short section of eroded, storm-battered cliffs. It's accessed from the coastal road towards Cala de Sant Vicent; look out for the sign in Castilian for "Aguas Blancas". The kilometre-long slice of dark sand here, interspersed with rocky outcrops and crumbling cliffs and buffeted by the ocean, is usually fairly empty, and the beach even offers a little surf some winters, although conditions are only ever ideal for a few days a year. Aigües Blanques is the only official nudist beach in the north of the island, and very popular with hippies, who gather at the *chiringuito* at the southern end of the shore – a favoured place to watch the sun rise over the Mediterranean.

Cala de Sant Vicent

Bus #23 from Santa Eulària, June–Sept 3 daily; May & Oct Mon–Fri 3 daily, Sat 1 daily; 40min. Ibiza's isolated northeastern tip offers some of the island's most dramatic highland country, dominated by the plunging valley of Sant

▼AIGÜES BLANQUES

Vicent, west of the resort of Cala de Sant Vicent, the only tourist development in this near-pristine area. Getting there is an attraction in itself: the coastal road north of Aigües Blanques

▲ CAN CURREU

offers one of Ibiza's most magnificent drives, following the corrugated coastline and weaving through thick pine forests, with sparkling waters offshore. Three kilometres after Aigües Blanques you catch a glimpse of Cala de Sant Vicent, its sweeping arc of golden sand enclosed by the 303-metre peak of **Sa Talaia** to the north, and steep cliffs to the south. Unfortunately, property developers have filled Cala de Sant Vicent's shoreline with a row of ugly concrete hotels, but the waters here still offer some of the best swimming in the area. Minimarts, cafés and restaurants sit below the hotels on an otherwise featureless promenade, while behind the prom stand the derelict remains of a **concrete house**, which served as the hideout of French assassin Raoul Villian after he killed the socialist leader Jean Jaurès in 1914 and fled to Ibiza. Villian lived here in near-total seclusion for almost two decades before he was finally tracked down and murdered in 1936.

Cova des Cuieram

June–Sept Tues–Sun 10am–2pm; call ☎971 301 900 for winter opening information. Free. A kilometre inland from Cala de Sant Vicent there's a paved turn-off on the right (north) to the Cova des Cuieram, an important site of worship in Carthaginian times. Hundreds of terracotta images of the fertility goddess Tanit have been unearthed here, some of which are now displayed in the archeological museum in Ibiza Town (see p.58). Consisting of several small chambers, the modest cavern has had to be structurally strengthened after damage inflicted some decades ago by a treasure-seeking lunatic armed with dynamite. Inside there's very little to see, though it's thought the stalactites could have been part of the cult of worship.

Sant Vicent

Ibiza's smallest village, Sant Vicent, 3km up the valley from the coast on the road to Sant Joan, is easily missed. Consisting of a handful of houses and a fenced basketball court, there are no sights except for the modest, minimalist village **church**, built between 1827 and 1838, with a double-arched porch and an appealing setting in its own tiny plaza, with a solitary palm tree for company. The facade is unembellished except for a small plaque, which confidently proclaims in Castilian Spanish: "house of God and gate to heaven". Around two hundred metres downhill from the church is Sant Vicent's only other feature, an orderly, dark little bar, *Es Café*, which also functions as the valley's post office and shop.

Port de ses Caletes

A tiny pebbly cove, barely 50m across, Port de ses Caletes is reachable only via a tortuous (but signposted) road from Sant Vicent that ascends via switchbacks to 250m and then plummets to the sea; it's a bumpy fifteen-minute drive from the village. With a ramshackle collection of dilapidated fishing huts as its only buildings, the cove is dwarfed by soaring coastal cliffs, and it's a blissfully peaceful spot, where there's nothing much to do except listen to the waves wash over the smooth stones on the shore or snorkel round the rocky edges of the bay.

Hotels

Can Curreu

☎ & ☎971 335 280, ⊛www.cancurreu.com. Converted *finca* high in the hills 2km west of San Carles and near *Las Dalias* bar (see p.92). The immaculate, commodious rooms all have private terraces, Jacuzzis, satellite TV, hi-fi, air con and open fires in winter; the suites (€320–395) are even grander, all with separate lounge areas. The beautiful grounds contain citrus groves, a cactus garden and a stable (horse riding available at €22 an hour). There's also a restaurant, pool and gym. Rates drop a little in winter. €235–258.

Can Pere

1km northwest of Roca Llisa golf course ☎971 196 600, ⊛www.canperehotel.com. Stunning, very tastefully converted nineteenth-century farmhouse, situated in supremely tranquil hilly countryside, yet just 7km north of Ibiza Town. The nine immaculate, attractive rooms all have air con and modish bathrooms, while the three suites (€155–211), all with separate lounge rooms, are very spacious and have real character; there's a magnificent pool too. Attentive, friendly staff. Breakfast is included, and evening meals are available. Rates drop to very reasonable levels in winter. €123–158.

Can Talaias

2km northwest of Cala Boix ☎971 335 742, ⊛www.hotelcantalaias.com. Wonderful rural hotel, owned by actor Terry-Thomas's son

▼CAN PERE

and his family, perched on a remote hilltop, with panoramic views over pine woods to the east coast. There's a slightly bohemian ambience – the stylish decor includes *objets d'art*, Asian fabrics and quirky sculptures. The seven rooms and suites (the latter starting at €270) are rich in character and comfort and have air con and satellite TV. Terrific sun terrace and a lovely pool area; breakfast is included and other meals are available. €140.

Ca's Català

c/del Sol, Santa Eulària ☎ 971 331 006, ⊛ www.cascatala.com. May–Oct. Friendly, English-run hotel set on a quiet street in the heart of Santa Eulària, close to restaurants, shops and beaches. The twelve (mostly en-suite) rooms are comfortable but not elaborately furnished, and there's a delightful courtyard shaded by palms, with a small pool and sun terrace. Breakfast is available (€8) and afternoon tea and cakes are served. No children. €75.

Hostal Cala Boix

Platja Cala Boix ☎ 971 335 224. Peacefully located above lovely Cala Boix beach, the sixteen simple, comfortable rooms here (all with air con and TV) have either mountain or sea views and offer excellent value. Breakfast is included and half-board rates are also available. €49.

Hostal Rey

c/Sant Josep 17, Santa Eulària ☎ 971 330 210. May–Oct. Pleasant, central, neat and tidy hotel where the twenty moderately

priced singles and doubles are all en suite, and have fans. Breakfast (not included) is served in the downstairs café. €53.

Campsites

Camping Cala Nova

Cala Nova ☎ 971 331 774, ⊜ campingcalanova@hotmail.com. Easter–Oct. Well-equipped site, 100m from Cala Nova beach and a short walk from Es Canar. Attractive, self-contained log cabins and mobile homes sleep two (€41–53) to six (€83–106).

Camping Vacaciones Es Canar

Es Canar ☎ 971 332 117. April–Oct. Popular with families, this site is close to the beach in the resort of Es Canar and has good facilities: a pool, laundry, security boxes and a bar/restaurant. Prices for the cabins (up to €28), caravans (up to €62) and hire tents (up to €18) depend on the season.

Cafés

Anita's

Sant Carles. Daily noon–1am. Highly atmospheric village inn that was once *the* gathering point

▼ ANITA'S

▲ C/SANT VICENT, SANTA EULÀRIA

for northern Ibiza's hippies. Still attracts a mixed bunch of local characters for the good *tapas* and full meals; enjoy them in the snug bar or on the vine-shaded patio.

Restaurants

Brasserie Dédé

c/Sant Vicent 25, Santa Eulària ☎971 332 210. May–Oct daily 1–3.30pm & 7pm–midnight. This is a good moderately priced French bistro-style place, at the western end of Santa Eulària's restaurant strip, with an excellent-value set meal (€10 for two courses) and plenty of à la carte choice. There's an attractive interior or you can dine at one of the pavement tables.

El Bigotes

Cala Mastella. May–Oct daily, Nov–April weekends only. Food served at 2pm only. No phone reservations; essential to book at least a day ahead in person. With (shared) wooden tables set right by the water's edge, this delightful lunch-only place

is one of Ibiza's most idyllic places to dine – it's just out of sight from the beach, around the rocks on the north side of the cove. There's not much choice: *bullit de peix* (fish and potato stew, with rice), grilled squid or fish, a basic wine list, but great Sa Caleta coffee. Count on about €25 per person.

Restaurant La Noria

Cala Boix ☎971 335 397. Daily 12.30–4pm & 8pm–midnight. Looking over Cala Boix beach and the Med, with tables placed under the clifftop pines, this informal, moderately priced place serves up excellent seafood: specialities include grilled squid, paella, *calderata de langosta* (lobster broth) and *guisado de pescado* (fish stew).

Restaurant Salvadó

Pou des Lleó ☎971 187 879. Daily 1–3.30pm & 7.30–11.30pm. In an isolated position overlooking an undeveloped fishing bay, *Salvadó* serves some of the freshest fish in the east at fair prices – expect to pay €25–30 per person including drinks. The paella and *bullit de peix* are especially good, and the service is friendly.

Bars

Café Guaraná

Port Esportiu, Santa Eulària ⊛www. guarana-ibiza.com. May–Oct daily 10pm–6am; Nov–April Sat & Sun 9pm–4am. Santa Eulària's premier bar-club and a key venue in the north of the island. House music and dance mixes from residents and all the main Ibiza-based DJs, plus some live music including rock, jazz and blues bands.

Las Dalias

Santa Eulària–Sant Carles road km 12. Daily 8am–2.30am. Inimitable north Ibizan bar with a large main room, a good-sized garden terrace and a slightly schizoid clientele of farmers and hippies. Hosts the weekly "Namaste" evening on Wednesdays, an Indian-themed night with vegetarian food, live music and a psychedelic trance tent (until 5am), plus assorted rock and jazz events and a quirky Saturday market (see p.85).

▼LAS DALIAS MARKET

The northwest

From the tiny cove of Cala d'en Serra close to the island's northernmost tip to the diminutive village of Santa Agnès, rugged northwest Ibiza is the wildest, most isolated part of the island. A soaring, almost unbroken range of towering cliffs and forested peaks, the coastline only relents to allow access to the shore in a few places. Just two bays – Port de Sant Miquel and the small family resort of Portinatx – have been developed for tourism. Elsewhere, the pristine and often deserted coast offers better hiking than beachlife, as well as terrific snorkelling. Inland, the thickly wooded, but sparsely populated terrain is interspersed with small patches of farmland where olives, carob, almonds, wheat and citrus fruits are nourished by the rust-red earth. Only picturesque Sant Joan and sleepy Sant Miquel here could realistically be described as villages, though all the other hamlets have a whitewashed church and a bar or two. Ancient Ibizan rural customs, including water dance rituals at remote springs and wells, still continue while traditional cuboid Ibizan *casaments* outnumber modern villas in many places. In the village bars the Ibizan dialect of Catalan, rather than Castilian Spanish, remains the dominant tongue.

Sant Joan

Bus #20 from Ibiza Town, May–Oct Mon–Fri 5 daily, Sat & Sun 2 daily; 35 min. Bus #21 from Santa Eulària, May–Oct Mon–Fri 2 daily; 20min. High in the northern hills the pretty village of Sant Joan (San Juan in Castilian) lies on the main highway from Ibiza Town to Portinatx, 22km from the capital. Though only a couple of hundred people live here, the village is a municipal capital and boasts its own modest little **Ajuntament** (Town Hall).

Dominating the skyline, the eighteenth-century **church**, just off the main highway, displays typically high, whitewashed walls and an arched side porch. The slim steeple that rises slightly awkwardly from the main body of the building is a twentieth-century addition, which detracts a little from the wonderfully minimalist simplicity of the original design. Inside, there's an unadorned single nave, with a barrel-vaulted roof and a small dome,

Transport

In summer infrequent **buses** run to (virtually) every village and resort in the northwest from Ibiza Town, plus the odd service from Sant Antoni; but very few buses operate in winter. You really need your own transport to properly explore this region.

The northwest PLACES

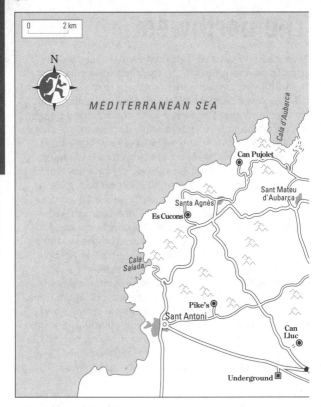

0   2 km

N

MEDITERRANEAN SEA

Cala d'Aubarca

Can Pujolet

Sant Mateu d'Aubarca

Santa Agnès

Es Cucons

Cala Salada

Pike's

Sant Antoni

Can Lluc

Underground

comprising several segments painted with images of Christ.

Though once an important hippy hangout (see box), evidence of Sant Joan's counter-cultural leanings is somewhat muted today; the spirit survives to an extent in the New Age-ish *Eco Centre* café in the heart of the village (see p.105). The region remains popular with a bohemian bunch of artists and writers, however, and the remote terrain around the village is a favoured destination for Ibiza's clandestine psychedelic trance party scene.

Hippy mecca

Sant Joan first became a focal point for northern Ibiza's **hippies** in the 1960s, when a scene developed around the legendary Can Tiruit commune. Later it served as a primary base for the Bhagwan Rajneesh cult (subsequently renamed the Osho Commune International), where elements of Sufism, Buddhism, Zen and yoga were blended with a good dose of hedonistic sexual libertinism. Rave folk history has it that Bhagwan Rajneesh devotees from California were the first people to bring ecstasy to Ibiza in the late 1970s, when there was the first mass ritual use of the drug on the island.

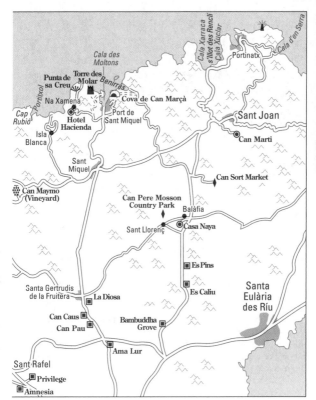

Xarraca Bay

Bus #20 from Ibiza Town, May–Oct Mon–Fri 5 daily, Sat & Sun 2 daily; 45min. North of Sant Joan, the main highway to Portinatx wriggles down to the coast following a beautiful, fertile valley flanked by olive-terraced hills and orderly almond and citrus groves. The route affords sweeping views of Xarraca Bay below, one of Ibiza's most expansive at 2km wide. Dotted with tiny rocky islands, the

▼CALA XARRACA

▲FUN ON THE BEACH AT PORTINATX

translucent waters are backed by low cliffs, and there are three small beaches. Four kilometres along the road from Sant Joan, a signposted side road loops past some villas to quiet **Cala Xarraca**, a thin strip of coarse sand and pebbles no more than 150m long, with a few sunbeds and umbrellas to rent. The solitary bar/restaurant sells full meals and tapas, and is a fine spot to watch cormorants, and spear-fishermen diving at the end of the day.

A kilometre further along the Portinatx road, **s'Illot des Renclí** is a beautiful thirty-metre-wide patch of well-raked sand and very shallow, azure water; just offshore is the tiny islet after which the beach is named. There's a decent fish restaurant here but no snacks are available. A further kilometre to the east, **Cala Xuclar** is a gorgeous sandy, horseshoe-shaped inlet sprinkled with fishing huts, plus an excellent *kiosko* (June–Oct) for meals and drinks. The beach is very tranquil and the waters offer excellent snorkelling possibilities.

Portinatx

Bus #20 from Ibiza Town, May–Oct Mon–Fri 5 daily, Sat & Sun 2 daily; 50 min. At the end of the highway, moderately sized, low-rise Portinatx is one of Ibiza's more attractive resorts. Set around a double bay, with three small sandy beaches and well-spaced hotels and apartment blocks between mature pines, it's a friendly, family-oriented holiday centre, with several other good beaches nearby. There's one stylish bar (*Zulu Lounge*; see p.107), but the restaurants tend to serve up standard-issue, tourist-geared fodder.

The larger of the bays, Port de Portinatx, has two golden patches of sand, **s'Arenal Gross** and **s'Arenal Petite**, where rows of sunbeds are rotated on an hourly basis in high season. The other beach, **Es Portitxol**, at the end of a narrow inlet 500m west of s'Arenal Gross, has well-sheltered water, perfect for swimming and snorkelling; there's also a dive school here (see p.169).

Cala d'en Serra

East of Portinatx, a very scenic road rises above Ibiza's northern tip, threading through woods and past isolated luxury villas. After 3km, there's a magnificent view of diminutive Cala d'en Serra, a remote, exquisite cove framed by green hills; it's reachable via a poor, signposted, but just about driveable dirt road. The only scar in the scenery is the ugly, half-built concrete shell of an abandoned hotel project just above the beach – though there are plans to demolish it soon. The bay's alluring, translucent waters make an idyllic place for a dip, and offer rich snorkelling around the rocky fringes of the inlet; it's a short swim across to another tiny pebbly cove (also accessible over the rocks to the south). A café-shack (May–Oct) just off the beach serves decent seafood, *bocadillos* and drinks.

Balàfia

The historic hamlet of Balàfia is characterized by its castle-like defence towers and is often cited as Ibiza's only surviving Moorish village, though the only thing definitely Arabic about the place is its name. Certainly one of the most

▼BALÀFIA

unusual settlements on the island, it contains a cluster of ancient, interlocking whitewashed houses, and ochre-coloured towers where the population once sheltered from pirates. Though there are a few "*Privado*" (private) signs, there's nothing to stop you walking around the hamlet's two alleys to get a closer look at the houses and towers. Close by, the **Can Sort** organic food market, a fairly modest affair, is held each Saturday in the hills between Sant Joan and Balàfia. To get there from the highway, take the turn-off signposted for the "Mercado del Campo" at km 11.9.

Sant Llorenç

A kilometre west of Balàfia, remote Sant Llorenç (San Lorenzo in Castilian) is one of Ibiza's least-visited settlements. There's nothing here but a couple of village bars, a handful of houses and a large whitewashed **church** that seems out of proportion with the rest of the place. A handsome eighteenth-century construction, it boasts a broad single-arched entrance porch lined with stone seating. Inside, the nave is topped with a barrel-vaulted roof, with a single nineteenth-century chapel dedicated to the Virgin Mary.

The wooded hillside above the church has been set aside as the **Can Pere Mosson country park**, a spacious recreation spot with good walking trails, barbecue areas and three lookout points offering fine views of the hilly heart of the island. The park is popular with Ibizan families at weekends, but deserted the rest of the week.

Benirràs

One of Ibiza's most idyllic beaches, Benirràs is a 300-metre-wide sandy cove set against a backdrop of high, densely forested cliffs. Development has been restricted here for decades, and buildings are currently limited to three unobtrusive beach restaurants (open May–Oct and some weekends in winter) and a handful of villas in the hills above. Legendary in Ibizan hippy folklore, and said to have been the site of wild drug-and-sex orgies in the 1960s, Benirràs's distinctly alternative tendencies persist today, and it remains the New Age community's favourite beach, as well as a centre for yoga (see p.171). Summer afternoons (particularly Sundays) see the bongo brigade gathering here to bang a drum at sunset. At the mouth of the bay lies **Cap Bernat** – a prominent rock islet that's somewhat revered by the spiritually minded. It's said to resemble, variously, a woman at prayer, a giant baby, or the Sphinx, however, in the cold light of day, it's difficult to see what all the fuss is about.

Sant Miquel

Bus #25 from Ibiza Town, May–Oct Mon–Sat 4 daily; Nov–April Mon–Sat 2 daily; 35min. Bus #22 from Sant Antoni, Tues & Thurs 2–3 daily; 40min. Bus #37 from Santa Eulària, Mon & Wed 2 daily; 25min. Perched high in the glorious Els Amunts hills, Sant Miquel is the largest of the villages in this region. It's not especially picturesque – the main street is lined with tiny old cottages that sit somewhat uneasily amongst five-storey apartment blocks – but it does retain plenty of unhurried, rural character, and you'll find a

good mix of locals and visitors in the bars during the summer.

The settlement dates back to the thirteenth century, when the first walls of a fortified church were constructed on the Puig de Missa hilltop, a defensive position some 4km from the sea, giving the original inhabitants a little extra protection from marauding pirates. It's a short, signposted stroll from the village's main street to the small plaza in front of the church, which commands magnificent views over the pine forests and olive groves, and has a small, welcoming bar. You enter the **Església de Sant Miquel** via the arches of a walled patio, then pass through a broad porch, which leads into the southern side of the barrel-vaulted nave. The recently restored frescoes of the Benirràs chapel, to the right of the altar, are the church's most unusual feature

▼ESGLÉSIA DE SANT MIQUEL

▲COVA DE CAN MARÇÀ

– swirling monochrome vines and flowers that blanket the walls and ceiling, dating back to the late seventeenth century, when construction was finally completed. Below the frescoes is some superb stonework of tessellated crosses and octagons. *Ball pagès* (folk dancing) displays are staged in the church patio every Thursday all year round (May–Oct 6.15pm; Nov–April 5.15pm; €3.50).

Port de Sant Miquel

Bus #25 from Ibiza Town, May–Oct Mon–Sat 4 daily; 40min. Bus #22 from Sant Antoni, Tues & Thurs 2–3 daily; 45min. Bus #37 from Santa Eulària, Mon & Wed 2 daily; 30min. From Sant Miquel, a scenic road meanders 4km north through a fertile valley to Port de Sant Miquel, a spectacular bay that was a tiny fishing harbour and a tobacco smugglers' stronghold until the 1970s. Craggy promontories shelter the inlet's dazzlingly blue, shallow waters, and there's a fine sandy beach, but the bay's beauty is tainted considerably by the portentous presence of two ugly concrete hotel blocks insensitively built into the eastern cliffs. Catering almost exclusively to the package tourist trade, Port de Sant Miquel's bars and restaurants are pretty average – the *Marin Dos* is the best with a decent *menú del día*, and, unlike all the others, open all year. In the summer season sarong and jewellery vendors set up stalls on the shore and pedalos are available for rent; you can also arrange boat trips to neighbouring beaches.

Cova de Can Marçà

Daily 11am–1.30pm & 3–5.30pm. Guided tours €5. Just past Port de Sant Miquel's monstrous hotels, Cova de Can Marçà is a modest-sized cave system that, though unlikely to get speleologists drooling with excitement, is the biggest in Ibiza. The cave is about 100,000 years old, and was formed by an underground river that once flowed through the hillside. There are some impressive stalactites and stalagmites, including one specimen that looks like a fat Buddha. An entertaining sound and light show ends the tour, with an artificial waterfall synchronized to cosmic electronic music from Tangerine Dream, who remain big in Ibiza.

Cala des Moltons

From the western edge of Port de Sant Miquel's beach, a path loops around the shoreline for 200m to a tiny cove, Cala des Moltons, where there's a small patch of sand and fine, sheltered swimming. The same trail continues past the beach for another kilometre, climbing through woods to a well-preserved stone defence tower, **Torre des Molar**, from where there are good views of the rugged northern coast towards Portinatx.

Na Xamena

Clinging to the vertiginous cliffs, and commanding spectacular vistas over the north shore, tiny Na Xamena consists of nothing more than a small development of holiday villas and the palatial *Hotel Hacienda* (see p.105). Nonetheless, if you're in the area it's worth a detour for the views alone, or for a quick drink in the hotel.

Swinging to the right just before the hotel, a bumpy

road heads north to the lofty peninsula of **Punta de sa Creu**, where a heliport serves the rich residents of the luxurious houses here. The panorama from the heliport is one of the most spectacular in all Ibiza; the jutting promontory is enveloped by the Mediterranean on three sides, and there's a brilliant perspective of the golden sands of Benirràs over in the east, and the mighty ochre cliffs around Portitxol and Cap Rubió just to the west.

Portitxol

Some 5km northwest of Sant Miquel, the hidden bay of Portitxol is one of the most dramatic sights in Ibiza – a fifty-metre-wide, horseshoe-shaped pebbly cove, strewn with giant boulders and dwarfed by a monumental backdrop of cliffs that seem to isolate the beach from the rest of the world. The only structures here are a ring of tiny stone-and-brushwood huts, owned by fishermen who use the bay as a sanctuary from the rough but rich waters, which plummet to over 90m in depth just a short distance from the beach. In high season, a few adventurous souls work

▼CLIFFS NEAR NA XAMENA

their way to this remote spot for a little secluded snorkelling, but for most of the year Portitxol is completely deserted, a pristine – but also sunbed- and refreshment-free – zone. There's plenty to explore, however: tracks skirt around colossal yellow boulders of earth and rock, and past weird rock formations; the craggy peak that looms 315m above the bay to the west is **Cap Rubió** (Blonde Cape), named for its sandy colour.

Getting to Portitxol is a bit tricky. From Sant Miquel, take the Sant Mateu road to the west, then after about a kilometre and a half, a turn on the right zigzags up through woods to the Isla Blanca complex of holiday villas. After you pass a kiosk (open June–Sept only) a rough road descends towards the shore. You'll soon reach a path that heads west by a high stone wall just before the second of two hairpin turns. Twenty minutes' more walking along the path, through some stunning cliffside scenery, and you're at the seashore, though for the very final descent you'll have to edge around the hillside for a short distance using the provided rope.

Sant Mateu d'Aubarca

There's little to the tiny village of Sant Mateu d'Aubarca, 7km west of Sant Miquel, other than a confusingly aimless collection of lanes, a solitary but friendly store-cum-bar and a typically well-fortified, whitewashed **church**. Completed in 1796, it has a fine triple-arched entrance porch and two tiny chapels, dedicated to the virgins of Montserrat and Rosario, set at the end of the draughtboard-tiled nave.

▲GRAPES, SANT MATEU D'AUBARCA

Tourism has barely touched the countryside around Sant Mateu, a rustic landscape of small fields of brick-red earth separated by low sandstone walls. Much of the land is given over to **vineyards**, and on the first weekend each December, the village hosts an annual festival in honour of the humble local *vi pagès* (country wine; see p.172). Less than a kilometre east of the village, just off the road to Sant Miquel, you can visit **Can Maymo** vineyard year-round; it produces 25,000 bottles of red and white wine annually and though they don't give tours they will sell you as many bottles as you can carry home.

Cala d'Aubarca

Once the main point of sea access for Sant Mateu, the untouched bay of Cala d'Aubarca, 4km north of the town, is one of Ibiza's most magnificent. In an island of diminutive cove beaches, its sheer scale is remarkable: a tier of cliffs towers above the three-kilometre-wide bay, and a choppy sea washes the rocky shoreline. There's no beach, and as a result, Cala d'Aubarca remains one of Ibiza's best-kept secrets, completely deserted for most of the year.

To get here from Sant Mateu, follow the road "Camí d'Aubarca" from the church; after 700m, you reach a junction. Bear left and follow the road through a large vineyard until you pass a white house with yellow windows on the right. Turn right just after the house, up a dirt road that leads to the wooded cliffs above Cala d'Aubarca. Past the cliffs, the road is in terrible condition, so you'll have to walk the final fifteen minutes down to the beach. When you reach the rugged promontory at the bottom of the dirt road, look out for the natural stone bridge carved out of the rock by the waves. With the sand-coloured formations of Cap Rubió to the northeast, and brilliant white patches of chalk at the back of the bay, the multicoloured cliffs are also striking.

Santa Agnès

Bus #30 from Ibiza Town, July–Sept Mon–Sat 3 daily; Oct–June Mon–Fri 1 daily; 35min. Bus #30 from Sant Antoni, July–Sept Mon–Sat 1 daily; 20min. Some 7km southwest of Sant Mateu, the tiny hamlet of Santa Agnès (Santa Inés in Castilian), is made up of a scattering of houses, a couple of streets, the simple *La Palmera* restaurant and the friendly *Can Cosmi* bar (see p.107). There are no specific sights other than

the village church, which dates from 1806. It's properly known as **Santa Agnès de Corona** (Saint Agnes of the Crown) – a reference to its location in the centre of a two-hundred-metre-high plain, enclosed by low hills on all sides which form a crown-like surround to the settlement. With a patchwork of small, stone-walled fields densely planted with figs, fruit and thousands of almond trees, the countryside here is very beautiful. If you visit in late January or early February, the sea of pink-white almond blossoms is an unforgettable sight.

Santa Gertrudis de la Fruitera

Bus #25 from Ibiza Town, May–Oct Mon–Sat 4 daily; Nov–April Mon–Sat 2 daily; 20min. Bus #22 from Sant Antoni, May–Oct Tues & Thurs 2–3 daily; 25min. Smack in the centre of the island, 11km from Ibiza Town and just off the highway to Sant Miquel, lies Santa Gertrudis de la Fruitera ("of the fruits" – the village is known for its crops of apples, apricots, peaches and oranges). It is a small but interesting settlement with an international – and rather bourgeois – character, and offers a glut of bars, restaurants and boutiques out of all proportion to its size. Even in the winter months, tank-like 4WDs and ancient Citröen 2CVs compete for prime parking positions, and a collection of moneyed expats (particularly Germans), farmers, artists and artists-who-farm fill the streetside café terraces of *Bar Costa* (see p.107), *Es Canto* and *Otto Cappuccini* (see p.105).

Besides the bars and boutiques offering ethnic fabrics, trinkets and handicrafts, there's also an excellent **auction house**,

Santa Agnès coastal hike

This circular walk (4.5km; 2hr) explores some of Ibiza's most remote coastal scenery, along high cliffs and through thick forest, and offers (if you're nimble) the chance of a dip in the sea. There are no refreshments along the route.

From the church in Santa Agnès, follow the paved Camí des Pla de Coruna road west past villas, farmhouses and fields of vines, fruit and almond trees divided by dry-stone walls. It's fifteen minutes to the *Can Jordi* restaurant (where you can park). Just before the restaurant there's a rough dirt track on the right that leads downhill to the sea. Follow this track, ignoring the first path on the left after a few metres, and continue down the track towards the waves, taking the next path on your left – it's about 200m from the road. This path continues southwest around the coastal cliffs, dotted with scrub pine and juniper bushes, keeping about 100m above the sea. The trail splits in places, but blue arrows mark the correct way, passing through the rocky headland of **Cap Negret** after another ten minutes' walking. Follow the blue arrows around a wall and the trail then continues through overgrown farm terraces before descending to a lovely clearing in the pines, where there's a long-abandoned farmhouse; the small domed stone structure was once a bread oven. Continuing west, you'll pass through a clump of giant reeds, then reach a series of large, overgrown farm terraces, propped up by substantial stone walls. Walk through the terraces past some old water storage tanks. The route is very close to the sea here, but you'll have to scramble down the rocks for a dip. To return, blue arrows direct you inland up the wooded hillside. The steep route is a little ill-defined at first, but soon joins a dried-up stream bed before continuing up a pine-clad valley. After fifteen minutes the trail levels out and descends gently to the Camí des Pla de Coruna; turn left, and it's a five-minute walk back to *Can Jordi*, or twenty minutes to Santa Agnès.

PLACES The northwest

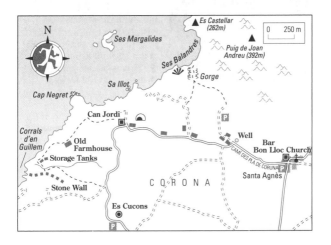

the English-owned Casi Todo (℡971 197 023; ⓦwww .casitodo.com; check website for auction days), where everything

from gypsy carts and antiques to rusty 1950s motorbikes go under the hammer once a month.

The landmark eighteenth-century **Església de Santa Gertrudis**, in the centre of the village, is less austere than most Ibiza churches, with an elevated frontage and small windows picked out with yellow paint. The interior, though hardly ornate, does have a few sculptural decorations, including, appropriately, some apples and figs on the ceiling.

On the outskirts of the village on the road to Sant Mateu, there's another chichi group of stores, including Nino d'Agata, a pricey boutique that specializes in jewellery and sculpture, and the well-stocked Casa Azul bookstore. The village hosts an excellent annual fiesta on November 16.

▼CASI TODO AUCTION HOUSE

Hotels

Can Marti

2km south of Sant Joan ☎971 333 500, ✆www.canmarti.com. March–Oct. Delightfully rustic family-run hotel (also operating as an eleven-hectare organic farm) set in a remote northern valley. The accommodation comprises two doubles, a studio apartment (€105) and a cottage sleeping four (€155); all exude charm and a certain bohemian style. Rates include bicycle hire; breakfasts are extra. €95.

Can Pla Roig

Sant Joan, just north of the church ☎ & ✆971 333 012. This very inexpensive Ibizan-owned guesthouse has simply furnished rooms, with shared or private bathroom; some rooms have their own terraces. There's also a communal kitchen. €34.

Can Pujolet

2.5km northeast of Santa Agnès ☎971 805 170, ✆www.ibizarural. com. Luxuriously converted farmhouse in a tranquil location in the hills above Santa Agnès. All accommodation, which includes suites (€259–305) and a bungalow (€281–310), is furnished with antiques and has air con; you can also make use of the huge pool and Jacuzzi. No restaurant, but breakfast is included. €171–209.

Casa Naya

Ibiza Town–Portinatx road, km 16.5 ☎971 325 264, ✆www.ibiza-spotlight. com/casanaya. Fine rural hotel in a renovated *finca* just south of Balàfia, with great views of Ibiza's forested northern hills. The nine rooms and suite (the latter costing €150–240) all have air con and private bathroom, and while the decor may be a little old-fashioned, the location and facilities make this very good value (especially outside high season). Also has a tennis court, gym and wonderful pool. €98–139.

▲ ES CUCONS

Es Cucons

2km southwest of Santa Agnès ☎971 805 501, ☎971 805 510, ⓦwww. escucons.com. One of Ibiza's finest rural hotels, with a wonderfully peaceful setting in the high inland plain of Santa Agnès. All the fourteen rooms and suites (the latter starting at €242) in the converted seventeenth-century farmhouse are very comfortable, with sabina pine-beamed ceilings, countryside views and all mod cons including air con and satellite TV; some have fireplaces and CD/DVD players. There's also an excellent restaurant, pool and lovely gardens. €214–240.

Hostal Cas Mallorquí

Es Portitxol, Portinatx ☎971 320 505, ☎971 320 594. Attractive beachside hotel in quiet Es Portitxol bay, with nine modern, comfortable and spacious rooms; all have sea views, TV, private bathrooms and air con or heating. There's a reasonable restaurant downstairs. €88.

Hotel Hacienda

Na Xamena ☎971 334 500, ⓦwww. hotelhacienda-ibiza.com. May–Oct. Ibiza's only five-star hotel, popular with supermodels and the seriously minted, set in a spectacular remote location high above the rugged northwest cliffs. The rooms are commodious, most with terraces and a Jacuzzi aligned for sunset-watching, and there are four restaurants, three swimming pools, a gym and a sauna/spa. Palatial suites also available (€432–712). €200–364.

Cafés

Eco Centre

Sant Joan. Mon–Sat 11am–9pm. Part New Age bazaar (complete with Osho music CDs and cactus plant drums) part Internet café, where northern Ibiza's hairy crew gather to surf, snack, sup and generally wallow in pre-punk nostalgia. There's also a lovely back garden.

Otto Cappuccini

Santa Gertrudis. Daily 9am–5pm. Very chic new café-restaurant, with metropolitan-style decor and furnishings (plus a glass floor that showcases the artistic owner's remarkable terracotta seabed sculpture). There are à la carte breakfast options, including great fresh juices and pastries, and a highly popular lunchtime salad buffet for €7.80 per person. The delicious bread is baked on the premises.

Restaurants

Ama Lur

Ibiza Town–Santa Gertrudis road, km 2.3 ☎971 314 554. Daily 12–4pm & 8pm–12.30am. Always very close to the top of the Ibiza chefs' own annual "Best Restaurant" vote, the renowned, and expensive *Ama Lur* serves superb Basque and Spanish cuisine in a formal setting with plenty of fish, seafood and interesting meat dishes. The waiting staff also really make an effort to look after the diners here.

Bambuddha Grove

Ibiza Town–Sant Joan road, km 8.5 ☎971 197 510, ⊛www.bambuddha. com. May–Oct daily 8pm–1.30am; Nov–April Thurs–Sun 7pm–1pm. Simply stunning pyramid-roofed restaurant, built by Balinese craftsmen from timber, thatch and bamboo, where the quality of the inventive "Mediterrasian" cooking – including tuna steak with wasabi, and a €28 Thai buffet – can be inconsistent. (Budget around €45–50 to eat à la carte.) The whole *Bambuddha Grove* experience, however, still offers a great night out, with candlelit tables overlooking lush gardens, and a funky bar area where DJs spin tunes until 4am.

Can Caus

Ibiza Town–Santa Gertrudis road, km 3.5 ☎971 197 516. July & Aug daily 1–4pm & 7.30pm–midnight. Specializing in local cuisine, particularly meat, this inexpensive place sources virtually all its produce, much of it organic, from the island. Feast on dishes such as cross-cut ribs or free-range chicken on bench seating outdoors, or in the snug interior.

Can Pau

Ibiza Town–Santa Gertrudis road, km 2.9 ☎971 197 007. June–Sept daily 8pm–midnight; Oct–May Tues–Sun 1–3.30pm & 8–11.30pm. Gorgeous converted farmhouse restaurant with a spacious dining area and a huge terrace overlooking a verdant garden. The Catalan cuisine includes plenty of meat choices including quails in cabbage leaf and a few fish dishes. Mains cost €13–22 each.

Cilantro

Santa Gertrudis, just south of the village church ☎971 197 387. May–Oct daily 1–4pm & 8pm–12.30am. Enjoyable, inexpensive garden restaurant with a short menu that includes tapas and mains such as great *pollo payes* (country chicken) and *gambas al ajillo* (prawns with garlic).

Es Caliu

Ibiza Town–Sant Joan road, km 10.8 ☎971 325 075. July & Aug 8pm–midnight; Sept–June daily 1–4pm & 8pm–midnight. A carnivore's paradise, this affordable and comfortable country restaurant serves superb grilled meat (and nothing else) to an almost exclusively Ibizan clientele. The decor is rustic, with the odd stag's head or stuffed fox on the whitewashed walls, and there's a pleasant terrace for the summer months. Book ahead on Sundays.

Es Pins

Ibiza Town–Sant Joan road, km 12 ☎971 325 034. Mon, Tues &

▲BAR COSTA

Thurs–Sun 1–4pm & 7.30–11.30pm. Very simple, inexpensive Ibizan restaurant with log-cabin decor. The spartan menu has island dishes such as the artery-challenging *sofrit pagès* (a kind of rustic Ibizan fry-up) and grilled meats. The three-course set-menu lunches are excellent value.

Bars

Bar Costa

Santa Gertrudis. Daily 8am–1am. Richly atmospheric village bar, with a cavernous interior and narrow, sociable pavement terrace. Legs of *jamón serrano* garnish the ceiling, while the walls are covered in paintings (most donated by artists to clear their bar bills). Decent menu and the most famous *tostadas* in Ibiza.

Cafeteria Es Pi Ver

Sant Miquel. Daily 7am–midnight. Uncontrived village bar – the 1970s Formica and fake wood decor aren't gunning for listed status approval, but the atmosphere is warm and welcoming. Decent tapas, country wine and beers.

Can Cosmi

Santa Agnès. Mon & Wed–Sun 11.30am–11pm. Famous throughout Ibiza for serving the island's finest *tortilla*, *Can Cosmi* is also a great local bar, with a convivial atmosphere, plenty of local characters, very moderate prices and good service. The elevated terrace is ideal for summer drinking, with fine views of the village church.

▲TORTILLA, CAN COSMI

Zulu Lounge

s'Arenal Petite, Portinatx. May–Oct daily 10am–1am). Almost hip bar-restaurant with agreeable chillout sounds and alcove tables set under the rockface that forms the rear of the bay. There's an extensive cocktail list, and menu of Mexican and Mediterranean dishes.

Clubs

La Diosa

Ibiza Town–Sant Joan road, km 3.7. June–Sept. Very welcome addition to the Ibiza scene, though most local residents were dead against the premises' conversion from a tacky Wild West theme eatery to today's chic club-cum-bar-cum-restaurant. The owners have created a visually stunning venue with a wonderfully verdant bar terrace and garden area, while the seriously stylish separate club interior is soundproofed. When well patronized, *La Diosa* ("The Goddess") offers a mighty location for a proper Balearic night out: drinking or eating under the stars before some serious dancefloor action. However, at the time of writing, the venue had yet to properly get going, so select your night out here with care. Sundays could be a good choice, when Zenith host parties with local DJs Reche and Carlos Díaz; look out for live music events too – renowned guitarist Paco Fernandez played at the venue several times in 2004.

Sant Antoni and around

The club-oriented scene in the package tourism resort of Sant Antoni (San Antonio) is as bombastic as you'll find in Europe. High-rise, concrete-clad and blatantly brash, San An (as it's usually called) primarily draws crowds of young clubbers bent on the relentless pursuit of unbridled hedonism, though it also finds room for some families too. Things can get out of control in the Brit-only enclave of the West End with its unbroken chain of bars, disco-bars and fast-food fryers, but there are less frenetic sides to the resort. On the west side of town there's a burgeoning array of stylish bars along the Sunset Strip and Caló des Moro, while Sant Antoni's harbour, prized by the Romans, remains the resort's best aspect – a sickle-shaped expanse of sapphire water that laps s'Arenal beach, backed by wooded uplands. Around Sant Antoni, away from the crowded sands at the heart of the resort, you'll find some impressive cove beaches, as well as plenty of other gorgeous swimming spots.

The harbourfront

Sant Antoni's main harbourfront begins at the **Egg**, a white sculpture erected to honour a tenuous claim that Christopher Columbus was born on the island. Inside the hollow structure is a miniature wooden caravel, modelled on the fifteenth-century vessels in which the explorer sailed. West of the Egg, the broad promenade has a luxuriant collection of tropical palms, rubber plants and flowering shrubs and a series of flashy modern fountains, dramatically illuminated at night. Behind the promenade is a string of concrete office and apartment blocks occupied at street level by rows of pavement cafés, where you can eat American fast food or tuck into a full English breakfast

Arrival and information

Buses all depart from stops at the western end of Passeig de la Mar. Bus #3 serves Ibiza Town (May–Sept 55 daily, plus nightbuses; Oct–April 29 daily, 25min) and bus #8 also runs there via Sant Josep (Mon–Sat 5 daily, Sun 2 daily, 30 min). **Boats** (all May–Oct only) depart from the harbourfront on Passeig de ses Fonts.

Sant Antoni's **tourist information** office (May–Oct Mon–Fri 9.30am–2.30pm & 3–8.30pm, Sat & Sun 9.30am–1pm; Nov–April Mon–Sat 9.30am–1pm; ☎971 314 005) is on the harbourfront, just west of the Egg.

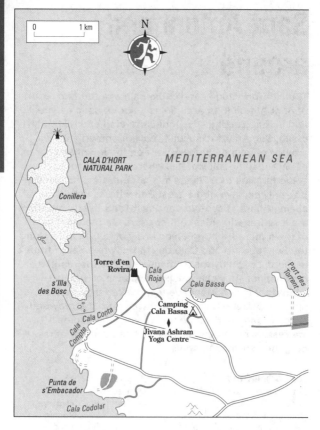

while gazing at a Mediterranean harbour. On summer evenings, this area is lined with street sellers and caricaturists, and filled with drinkers.

The promenade narrows once you've passed a statue of a fisherman, complete with nets and catch; opposite here is the **Moll Vell**, the old dock, where you'll often see fishermen mending their nets and fixing reed lobster pots. Further west, you pass the marina and modern Club Nautic (Yacht Club) building and the main bus terminal before you reach a 400-metre-long dock that juts

into the harbour, from where huge ferries head for mainland Spain.

Església de Sant Antoni

Just north of the harbourfront up c/Ample is the large Església de Sant Antoni, a handsome, whitewashed structure with a twin belfry and a pleasantly shady side porch. The building mainly dates from the late seventeenth century, though there has been a chapel here since 1305. It has an unusual rectangular defence tower built into its southeast flank; until the early nineteenth century,

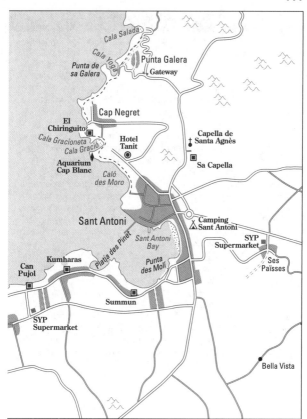

cannons were mounted at the top of this tower to defend the town from marauding pirates. You approach the church through the twin arches of a cobbled, courtyard-like patio, with an elegant columned porch to the left. The sombre interior has little decoration, though some dark oil paintings of saints line the nave. The gilded altar replaced a previous Baroque piece destroyed during the Spanish Civil War.

The West End

The island's most raucous bar zone, the notorious West End

– described by writer Paul Richardson as "The Blackpool of Ibiza, cheerfully vulgar, unashamedly unglamorous"

▼BELLTOWER, ESGLÉSIA DE SANT ANTONI

Sant Antoni and around

The San An scene

San An's importance as a breeding ground for **dance music** talent is undeniable. All the main players who kickstarted the UK's acid house revolution in 1987 holidayed in the town, soaking up inspiration at key venues such as the *Project* and *Milk* bars which became bases for Chicago house music and Detroit techno, while the bars and clubs in virtually every other European resort were still playing party chart hits. Seduced by the spirit and vitality of the scene in San An and at *Amnesia*, the likes of Paul Oakenfold and Danny Rampling sought to re-create the energy back in London.

Meanwhile, the more eclectic cinematic sounds championed by José Padilla at the *Café del Mar* became the focus for an Ibizan **chillout scene** and CD series that influenced key producers and musicians all over the world, establishing Ibiza as an epicentre of electronic music.

By the mid-1990s, as clubbing became much more of a mainstream phenomenon, Ibiza's clubbing kudos and reputation for musical authenticity drew young British holidaymakers en masse to party in San An and experience the island's **unique scene**. The resort enjoyed its best years around the millennium, when over a dozen key UK clubs decamped to Ibiza for the summer and established residencies in San An and elsewhere on the island.

Today the innovation that unleashed acid house and a million chillout compilations is barely evident in San An, and though the odd new DJ talent does emerge, the music scene in the town has become pretty lifeless, with an army of young wannabe DJs playing almost identical funky house to the funky house-loving masses. San An barely picked up on the electroclash phenomenon tearing up underground London clubs in 2002 and 2003, while the R&B, breakbeat and hip-hop flavours that UK teenagers now identify with are pretty peripheral. Perhaps inevitably for a resort so interconnected with the dance music scene, this has lead to declining numbers of tourists, as Ibiza-style sounds and leading DJs can now be found at resorts throughout the Med.

– spreads over a network of streets centred around c/Santa Agnès. There's nothing subtle about this almost entirely British enclave of wall-to-wall disco-bars and pubs, interspersed with the odd hole-in-the-wall kebab joint or Chinese restaurant serving fry-up breakfasts. In summer the streets are overrun with sunburnt lager louts in football shirts; understandably, few Ibizans would dream of drinking around here and you'll be able to tell straight away if it's the kind of place you'll love or hate. In general drinks are much cheaper than Sunset Strip or Ibiza Town averages, and as the

▼WEST END

▲CALÓ DES MORO

disco-bars are usually free it's an inexpensive place to strut your stuff. The music is generally party-anthem holiday house and mainstream R&B, but plenty of decent DJs have cut their teeth in the better bars, which include the *Simple Art Club* and *Kremlin*, both on c/Santa Agnès.

The Sunset Strip

Stretching for 250m along the rocky shoreline between c/General Balanzat and c/Vara de Rey, Sant Antoni's legendary Sunset Strip of chillout bars is the most sophisticated side of the resort. In the day, the setting appears far from ideal – the bars cling to a jagged, low-lying rocky shelf and it's a tricky scramble over the rocks to take a swim. However, the location starts to make sense towards sunset, when all eyes turn west to watch the sun sinking into the blood-red sea, to a background of ambient soundscapes.

Until 1993, there was only one chillout bar, the ground-breaking *Café del Mar* (see p.123), along this entire stretch of coast which was very much

the preserve of in-the-know clubbers and islanders. But since then the scene has proliferated and there are half a dozen such bars here, with the sunset spectacle now very much part of most people's "Ibiza experience".

It's undeniable that the original vibe, created by José Padilla at *Café del Mar* and nurtured by a small clique of like-minded chillout DJs and producers, has been considerably diluted. The hype is incredible in the height of summer, when thousands of visitors congregate, television crews stalk the strip and web cams beam the sunset scene around the globe. The commercialism is unavoidable – all the bars now sell their own T-shirts and CD mixes – but in spite of these changes, a certain unique atmosphere does survive, especially early and late in the summer season, when things are less high-octane.

Caló des Moro

North of the Sunset Strip, the rocky shoreline continues for some 500m to Caló des Moro, a tiny cove with a small patch of

PLACES

Sant Antoni and around

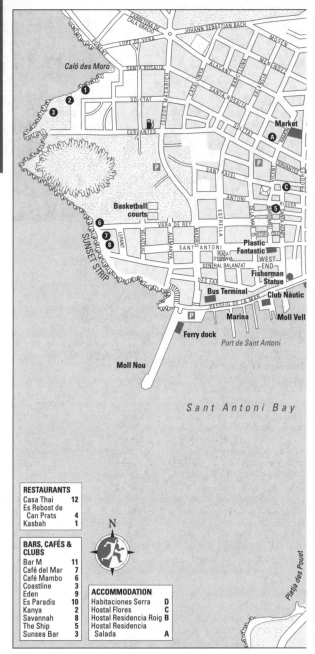

RESTAURANTS

Casa Thai	12
Es Rebost de Can Prats	4
Kasbah	1

BARS, CAFÉS & CLUBS

Bar M	11
Café del Mar	7
Café Mambo	6
Coastline	3
Eden	9
Es Paradis	10
Kanya	2
Savannah	8
The Ship	5
Sunsea Bar	3

N

ACCOMMODATION

Habitaciones Serra	D
Hostal Flores	C
Hostal Residencia Roig	B
Hostal Residencia Salada	A

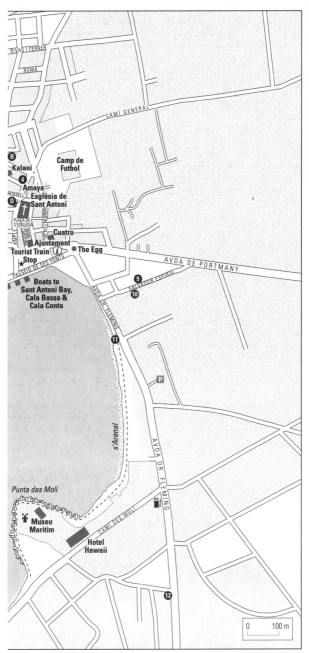

sand surrounded by a scattering of hotel and apartment blocks. The opening of several swanky new bar-restaurants here has helped Caló des Moro become San An's most happening location in recent years, rivalling the Sunset Strip as *the* premier chillout zone.

The bay makes an inviting place for a dip, with shallow, turquoise water. However, most people choose to patronize the swimming pools of the landmark shoreside bars at the sweeping modernist *Coastline*, *Sunsea Bar* and the neighbouring *Kanya*.

S'Arenal

South of the Egg, slimline s'Arenal beach hugs the shore as far as the Punta des Molí promontory. Though not the best beach in the area, as it's the nearest one to town, the sands get very busy in summer. A section of the sea is partitioned off from jetskiers and boats so that swimmers can enjoy themselves safely, while bordering the beach are some stylish bar-cafés including *Bar M* (see p.123). A landscaped, palm-lined harbourside promenade runs along the back of the bay.

Punta des Molí

Jutting into the harbourfront at the southern end of the promenade, past a row of block-like hotel complexes, is an imposing old white windmill with warped wooden sails which crowns the Punta des Molí promontory. This quiet, landscaped spot is planted with olive trees, lavender and rosemary bushes and is the site of the island's planned Museu Marítim (of uncertain opening date). Beside the fenced-off museum enclave, there's a restored well and an old water wheel, and panoramic views over the entire Sant Antoni bay.

Cala Gració

A kilometre northwest of Caló des Moro, around the rocky fringes of Sant Antoni bay, is the small but gorgeous beach of Cala Gració, an elongated patch of fine white sand which stretches back 100m from the sea. The shallow water is wonderfully calm and clear, and only gets really busy at the height of summer. A small snack bar rents out pedalos, sunbeds and umbrellas between May and October.

▼PUNTA DE SA GALERA

▲CALA SALADA

Aquarium Cap Blanc

Cala Gració is home to the modest Aquarium Cap Blanc (daily 10.30am–7pm; €3), set in an old smugglers' cave on the south side of the bay. The small aquarium is home to a collection of sluggish-looking Mediterranean sea life, including lobster, moray eels, wrasse and octopuses. It's well organized and popular with children, with wooden walkways above pools containing the sea creatures.

Cala Gracioneta

Bus #1 from Sant Antoni, May–Oct 12 daily; 10min. From the fishing huts on the north side of Cala Gració, a path clings to the shoreline, leading after 100m to a second hidden bay, the exceptionally beautiful and peaceful Cala Gracioneta. This little gem of a beach is barely 30m wide, but has exquisitely fine, pale sand, backed by pines; the shallow, sheltered waters here heat up to almost bathtub temperatures by late summer. The bay also boasts a wonderful restaurant, *El Chiringuito* (see p.122), where food is served practically on the sand.

Punta de sa Galera

North from Cala Gracioneta, the isolated bay of Punta de sa Galera (also known as Cala Yoga) is popular with naturists and hippies. Bizarre eroded cliffs of stratified stone and a series of shelf-like rock terraces (many painted with New Age doodles) form natural shelves for sunbathing, and the sapphire waters offer excellent snorkelling. In summer, a costume-less hippy sells cool drinks from an icebox most afternoons, and there's even a reiki masseur and reflexologist here, available (in theory) daily from 7pm to 8pm. To get to Cala Yoga by road, take the Cala Salada turn-off from the Sant Antoni–Santa Agnès highway, continue downhill until you reach a white arched gateway across the road, where the road splits; then bear left downhill towards the sea.

Cala Salada

Ringed by a protective barrier of steep, pine-clad hills, the small, all-but-undeveloped cove-beach of Cala Salada makes an idyllic escape from the crowds of Sant Antoni, with inviting turquoise waters lapping against a fine 100m strip of sand. Apart from a line of stick-and-thatch fishermen's huts, a solitary villa and a simple seafood restaurant, *Cala Salada* (May–Oct daily; Nov–April Sat & Sun), popular with locals, there's nothing here but the sea and beach. It is, however, one of the best places in the Pitiuses to watch the sunset, ideally in winter, when the sun sinks into the ocean between the gateway-like outlines of the islands of Conillera and Bosc.

▲COOLING OFF, CALA CONTA

To the north of Cala Salada, about two hundred metres across the bay, is an even more peaceful sandy cove, Cala Saldeta – you can either swim over or follow a path that winds around the fishing huts.

Sant Antoni bay

Buses #2 and #6 from Sant Antoni, May–Oct 48 daily plus nightbuses; Nov–April 22 daily; 20min. Boats from Sant Antoni, May–Oct hourly; 5–15min. Officially, the urban limits of Sant Antoni end at the Punta des Molí (see p.116). Continuing west you enter its "bay" area, which is a little less built-up. Plenty of British visitors booked on last-minute deals end up in hotels around Sant Antoni bay, and though the area is unremittingly touristy, it tends to attract more families than San An itself, so the atmosphere is less boisterous.

From the Punta des Molí promontory, c/de Cala de Bou heads west around the bay, between apartment and hotel blocks and the attendant commercial sprawl. The best beach on this stretch is **Platja des Pinet** (or Platja d'en Xinxó), some 3km west of Punta des Molí. It's certainly nothing special – a small sandy cove, barely 100m wide, but there's safe swimming

in the sheltered waters and three cheap shoreside snack bars. It's possible to waterski or take a ride on an inflatable banana here, and there's also a rickety-looking waterslide complex (May–Oct 9am–7pm; two rides €1, ten rides €3.50). The coastal road around Sant Antoni bay comes to a halt at the pretty sandy cove of **Port des Torrent**, named after a seasonal stream which originates on Ibiza's highest peak, Sa Talaiassa (see p.129), and empties into the small bay. Nestled at the end of a deep inlet, Port des Torrent's sands are packed with families lounging on sunbeds and splashing about in the calm water during the summer, when a snack bar-restaurant also opens; for the rest of the year, it's empty save for the odd fisherman.

Cala Bassa

Bus #7 from Sant Antoni, May–Oct 8 daily; 25min. Boats from Sant Antoni, May–Oct 5–7 daily; 25min. Cala Bassa is one of the most popular beaches in the Sant Antoni area: a fine, 250-metre-wide sandy beach set in a striking horseshoe-shaped bay, ringed by low cliffs and sabina pines. There are plenty of sunbeds and umbrellas to rent and three large café-restaurants, as well as a wonderful view of the hump-shaped coastal outcrop of Cap Nunó and the wooded hills of the island's northwest. The sparkling waters have been awarded Blue Flag status and there are plenty of watersports on offer, from waterskiing to banana rides, as well as a roped-off area for swimmers. Cala Bassa does tend to get very busy in high season, but peace returns and the beach clears by 7pm, when the last transport departs.

Cala Conta and Cala Compte

Bus #4 from Sant Antoni, May–Oct 8 daily; 25min. Boats from Sant Antoni, May–Oct 5–7 daily; 35min. After a three-kilometre loop around the remote rocky coastline of western Ibiza, the Cala Bassa road ends at the exposed beach of Cala Conta which, together with neighbouring Cala Compte, is generally considered one of Ibiza's very best. Though there are only two small patches of golden sand, it's easy to see why people rave about the place: gin-clear water, superb ocean vistas and spectacular sunsets. There's also a large café-restaurant behind the sands, selling fairly standard tourist-geared food.

Just to the north is the inlet of Cala Compte, where there are two more tiny sandy bays, one popular with naturists that has its own *chiringuito* for snacks. The island directly offshore is called **s'Illa des Bosc**, "Island of Woods", though it's now completely deforested, the trees having been felled for charcoal burning over a century ago. Only strong swimmers should attempt the 400-metre channel-hop to the island (when conditions are calm) as swift currents can sweep along this section of the coast.

The much larger island of **Conillera** just north of s'Illa des Bosc is visible from most points of Sant Antoni bay, from where its elongated profile resembles a giant beached whale. Many local legends are attached to the island – it's said to have been the birthplace of Hannibal and also to be the best source of the *beleño blanco* psychoactive herb, collected by pagan practitioners each year and burned during the night of Sant Joan (see p.172). Topped by a lighthouse, the island is uninhabited today.

Cala Codolar

Bus #4 from Sant Antoni, May–Oct 4 daily; 30min. About 2km south of Cala Compte, minuscule Cala Codolar is very pretty indeed, with fine, pale sand and clear waters sheltered by the rocky headland to the north, though it can get crowded in high season with tourists from the *Club Delfín* hotel just above the bay. There's a good seafood restaurant, *Restaurant Amarant*, and a windsurfing school, both open between May and October only.

▼CALA COMPTE

Sant Rafel

Bus #3 from Ibiza Town or Sant Antoni May–Sept 55 daily plus nightbuses; Oct–April 29 daily; 15min. Perched atop the central hills midway between Sant Antoni and Ibiza Town, just off the main highway, is the fairly featureless village of Sant Rafel, all but overshadowed by the mighty clubbing temples of *Amnesia* and *Privilege* close by to the south. The village does have a decent assortment of stores, cafés and several good restaurants, however, mostly strung out along its modest high street. There are also several ceramic workshops on the main drag. Local ceramics are also usually on show at the annual October 24 fiesta. Around 300m east of the high street is the nicest part of the village, centred around the **church**. Built between 1786 and 1797, it's typically Ibizan, with metre-thick whitewashed walls visible for miles around, and impressive buttresses. From the churchyard there are stunning views down to Dalt Vila and the sea.

Hotels

Can Lluc

Sant Rafel–Santa Agnés road, km 2 ☏971 198 673, ⊛www.canlluc.com. See map p.94. Set in a converted Ibizan *finca*, this luxurious rural retreat offers sumptious, characterful accommodation. Most of the twelve rooms have exposed stone walls and beams, while all have CD players, air con and sublimely soft beds and linen. The extensive gardens are also beautifully tended, and the large L-shaped pool is a wonderful place to while away the hours. Breakfast is included; other meals are available on request. €275.

Pike's

3km east of Sant Antoni ☏971 342 222, ⊛www.pikesibiza.com. See map p.94. One of Ibiza's most celebrated hotels, centred on a fifteenth-century farmhouse, *Pike's* combines a relaxed ambience with (perhaps slightly fading) celebrity cachet: Wham's "Club Tropicana" video was filmed here, while Freddie Mercury chose the hotel as his birthday venue. Other rural hotels may have usurped *Pike's* in the style stakes – the furnishings are looking a little dated – but the rooms are comfortable and have all mod cons. There's a selection of accomodation, with suites starting at €242, a good restaurant, swimming pool, sun terraces, a Jacuzzi, gym and floodlit tennis court. €185–203.

Pensions

Habitaciones Serra

c/de Rossell 13 ☏971 341 326. May–Oct. Run by a friendly Ibizan family, this simple guesthouse in a quiet location close to Sant Antoni's church has ten basic, tidy and very inexpensive rooms, all sharing bathrooms. €31.

Hostal Flores

c/de Rossell 26 ☏971 341 129. June–Sept. Centrally located hotel, with fairly large, comfortable rooms, all with private bathrooms, and a popular bar-café downstairs. €30.

Hostal Residencia Roig

c/Progress 44 ☏971 340 483. June–Sept. This pleasant *hostal* just north of the centre of San An is popular with young British visitors. The 37 attractive rooms have pine furnishings, good-quality beds and private bathrooms, and most have balconies. Guests can use a pool nearby. €52.

Hostal Residencia Salada

c/Soletat 24 ☎971 341 130. Easter–Oct. Spick-and-span small hotel, set on a quiet street, with budget singles and doubles, some with private balconies and bathrooms. €38.

Campsites

Camping Cala Bassa

Cala Bassa ☎971 344 599, ✉eccbassa@teleline.es. Beautiful site close to Cala Bassa beach, with full facilities, including a restaurant. Cabins sleeping two to four (€64), caravans sleeping six (€80) and hire tents (€5) are also available. Regular buses and boats run to and from Sant Antoni in the daytime, but you'll need your own transport or a taxi at night.

Camping Sant Antoni

Ctra Sant Antoni–Ibiza Town, km 1 ☎617 835 845. Pleasant shady spot, just a five-minute walk

from the Egg, though it can get noisy. One-bedroom bungalows are also available (€48 with bathroom, or €26 without), and discounts are available for stays of more than two weeks.

Shops

Amaya

Plaça de s'Església, Sant Antoni. Inexpensive trendy clothing and party-wear accessories.

Cuatro

c/Ramón i Cayal 4, Sant Antoni. Very select men's gear including Evisu and Maharishi, and friendly service.

Kalani

34Q c/del Progrés, Sant Antoni. Surf specialists with boards for hire, wet suits, clothing and accessories, plus good local advice about conditions.

Plastic Fantastic

c/Sant Antoni 15, Sant Antoni. One of San An's finest vinyl specialists, well stocked with all dance genres and selling some CDs too.

PLACES Sant Antoni and around

▼CALA BASSA

▲BAR M

Restaurants

Can Pujol

c/des Caló, Sant Antoni bay ☎971 341 407. Daily except Wed 1–3.30pm & 8pm–midnight; closed Dec–Jan 6. One of the most famous fish and seafood restaurants in Ibiza, particularly for lobster. The scruffy beach hut-style surroundings and furniture belie the quality and price – expect to pay €35–40 a head – of the cuisine. It's just east of Port des Torrent, with fine sunset views over the Mediterranean.

Casa Thai

Avgda Dr Fleming 34, Sant Antoni ☎971 344 038. May–Oct daily 11am–11pm. Authentic budget Thai diner offering a Bangkok-style setting, with neon-lit outdoor seating next to a fume-filled highway. Curries, stir-fries and noodle dishes are served up at a furious pace; the three-course set menu at €10.50 is a steal.

El Chiringuito

Cala Gracioneta ☎971 348 338. May–Oct daily 12.30–4pm & 8pm–12.30am. Sublime setting right by the water's edge in a sandy cove – it's especially pretty at night, when the restaurant owners float candles in the bay's sheltered waters. The straightforward moderately priced menu includes fish, paella and delicious barbecued meats, and there's a decent wine list.

El Clodenis

Plaça de s'Església, Sant Rafel ☎971 198 545. April–Oct daily 12.30–3.30pm & 8pm–1am. This excellent and expensive Provençal restaurant consistently delivers very high standards of cooking and offers an extensive wine list. It also enjoys a romantic setting opposite the whitewashed village church – book ahead for a terrace table in summer. The intimate dining rooms, decorated with Gallic prints, are also richly atmospheric.

Es Rebost de Can Prats

c/Cervantes 4, Sant Antoni ☎971 346 252. Daily 12.30–3.30pm & 7.30pm–midnight; closed Feb. Moderate. Very traditional family-owned Ibizan restaurant in a late nineteenth-century house with pleasingly old-fashioned decor and friendly service. Moderately priced dishes include pork rice, *calamars farcits* (stuffed squid) and local desserts.

Kasbah

Caló des Moro ℗971 348 364, ⊛www.kasbahibiza.com. May–Oct daily noon–1am. Overlooking the pretty bay of Caló des Moro, this enjoyable Ibiza bistro-style restaurant (owned by DJ Judge Jules) has an excellent, elevated setting. Fine global cuisine – based on the freshest ingredients – including dishes such as surf-and-turf brochette and Lebanese chicken. Expect to pay about €35 per person including drinks. The adjoining bar area is the ideal place for a pre-dinner apéritif or a post-nosh glass of Hierbas liqueur.

Sa Capella

Sant Antoni–Santa Agnès road, km 0.5 ℗971 340 057. April–Oct 8pm–1am. Set in an eighteenth-century chapel just off the Sant Antoni–Santa Agnès road, and patronized by the DJ elite and Ibiza's moneyed crowd, the highly evocative surroundings are the real attraction here, as the expensive Mediterranean

menu is perfectly competent if not exemplary.

Bars

Bar M

Avgda Dr Fleming, Sant Antoni. May–Oct daily 10am–3am. Owned by the Manumission team, this striking contemporary beach bar, just south of the Egg, is an essential pre-club venue, with storming live DJ mixes and performances from visiting bands. There's a huge outdoor terrace facing the beach, an upper deck and food too.

Café del Mar

Sunset Strip, Sant Antoni. April–Oct daily 5pm–1am Renowned bar that first put Ibiza on the map, the *Café del Mar* really should be on some kind of Balearic Beat heritage trail. Resident DJs maintain José Padilla's tradition of dreamy soundscapes, raising the tempo later with house grooves. Worth a visit, but sunset pilgrims beware that the slightly ridiculous mock baroque interior and location – beneath an unlovely concrete apartment block – is a letdown.

▼CAFÉ MAMBO

Café Mambo

Sunset Strip, Sant Antoni. May–Oct daily 11am–2am. Funky, music-geared bar with a stylish, canopied double-deck bar terrace with sun loungers and showers. DJs mix everything from nu jazz beats to classic bossa nova before ramping up the house music later in the day. Hosts a glut of pre-club parties, with big-name guest DJs.

Kanya

Caló des Moro, Sant Antoni. May–Oct daily 10am–4am. Set in a superb position right on the coast, this increasingly popular venue offers fine house DJs and some dance-floor action. Daytime snacks and meals are available, and there's a pool and sun terrace for daytime chilling.

Kumharas

c/Lugo, Sant Antoni bay. April–Oct daily 11am–3am. This is the only bohemian venue for miles around, despite its location in concrete packageland, and offers a radically different take on the standard sunset bar formula. There's global beats and ambient music, plenty of art and sculpture, a pan-Asian food menu and regular cultural events.

▲STATUE, KUMHARAS

Savannah

Sunset Strip, Sant Antoni. May–Oct daily 10am–2am. Triple-deck bar with an elegant hardwood interior, and an extensive terrace with sun loungers and brushwood brollies. DJs play placid daytime chillout tunes and Balearic house mixes after sundown. The funky lounge at the rear is open till 6am.

The Ship

Plaça de s'Era d'en Manyà. April–Oct daily 10am–3am. Friendly English-run pub serving British ale, popular with English bar and club workers. It's also a good source of information, with Internet access, plus noticeboards full of apartment rentals and jobs.

Sunsea Bar

Caló des Moro. April–Oct daily 10am–2am. Set beneath a sweeping Modernist apartment building, this bar, together with the neighbouring *Coastline*, has an extensive sun terrace, pools, rattan sofas and posh loungers. It's often booked for pre-club warm-ups but despite the surroundings, the atmosphere can be a little flat.

Underground

Ibiza Town–Sant Antoni road, km 7. June–Sept open selected evenings midnight–6am. See map p.94. This superb club-bar, set in a converted farmhouse just north of the main cross-island highway, attracts an older bunch of hip Ibizans and international faces. The large dancefloor has a potent sound system and there are adjacent lounge-around rooms and a beautiful garden terrace. Access is a bit tricky: be careful when making the U–turn off the main highway.

Clubs

Amnesia

Ibiza Town–Sant Antoni road, km 5
Ⓦ www.amnesia.es. June–Sept. See
map p.94. Musically, *Amnesia* is
the most influential club in
Ibiza, responsible for igniting
the whole British acid house
explosion and the resultant
global clubbing revolution. On
the right night, it can feel more
like a live gig than a nightclub,
with an audience of thousands
facing the DJ stage in the main
room, punching the air to
trance anthems – all under dry
ice-belching cannons.

The vast warehouse-like main
room is almost bereft of decor,
save a banner or two bearing
the promoter's logo, and its
huge dancefloor is ideally suited
to techno and hard house. In
contrast, the terrace occupying
the other side of the club is
topped by a graceful atrium
and beautified by lush greenery;
there's a dancefloor here, too,
but the music concentrates on
less intense vocal house and
Balearic rhythms. Forming an
upper level around both sides
of the club, the VIP balcony
has stylish contemporary
furnishings, Asian artefacts and
statues.

A lowly farmhouse thirty
years ago, *Amnesia* became
a hangout for hippies in the
1970s, with music ranging from
prog-rock to reggae and funk.
But after being completely
eclipsed by *Ku* in the early
1980s, *Amnesia* reinvented itself
as Ibiza's first after-hours club,
opening at 5am with eclectic
mixes spun by DJ Alfredo. By
1985 *Amnesia* was the most
fashionable club on the island
with an underground musical
policy that encompassed dark
hi-energy, minimal proto-house
tunes and electro Italian club
hits. This spirit of innovation has
ensured the club's continuing
success, and the owners have
proved adept at working with
key foreign promoters including
Cream and Sven Vath's Cocoon
while maintaining their own
espuma (foam) parties and
hosting one of the greatest
gay nights in Europe: La Troya
Asesina.

Eden

c/Salvador Espiriu, Sant Antoni Ⓦ www
.edenibiza.com. June–Sept. *Eden*
gives its loyal, young and mainly
British crowd exactly what
they want – a raver's delight
of pounding house and trance,
plenty of club anthems and
an orgiastic party atmosphere.
Though it's now Ibiza's most
modern venue, Eden was
considered a bit of a joke for
years – a disco throwback
that the leading DJs shunned.
However, serious investment
in 1999 and 2000 resulted in
state-of-the-art sound and
visual systems, a new industrial-
decor refit and multiple new
rooms, stages, bars and podiums.
BBC Radio One's Dave

▼EDEN

Pearce and Judge Jules were installed (and remain) resident DJs, and, boosted by massive support from punters, *Eden* assumed local supremacy, and has sustained this success. The club's unpretentiousness means that its never going to be the most fashionable place on the island, but it can claim to be top dog in San An, and achieved quite a coup by persuading the Ministry of Sound to relocate their Ibiza night to San An in 2004 from *Pacha*.

Eden's exterior is unmissable at night, bristling with electric-blue-lit domes and minarets. Twin steel serpents flank the lobby, while the interior is minimalist in design, with a huge main room under a domed roof; there's a chillout zone and a spacious back room playing alternative sounds. A Gaudí-esque steel balcony forms the substantial upper-level gallery, housing a White Room VIP zone, VJ booths and more bars.

Es Paradis

c/Salvador Espiriu, Sant Antoni
ⓦwww.esparadis.com. May–Oct.
Aesthetically, *Es Paradis* is one of the most stunning clubs in the Mediterranean, its square foundation topped by the venue's retractable roof, a beautiful glass pyramid which dominates the skyline of Sant Antoni bay. The second oldest of the big Ibizan clubs, it will celebrate its thirtieth anniversary in 2005. The core crowd here is young British San An-based holidaymakers bent on a great night out – not a particularly cosmopolitan scene, but they sure know how to enjoy themselves.

Inside, though the decor remains immaculately looked after, the disco-era design of neo-Greco columns, marble flooring and verdant foliage is looking a little dated. Nevertheless there are ten bars, a giant tropical fish tank, podium dancers and awesome sound and light systems, while encircling the entire building, the upper balcony contains a second room with alternative sounds.

The club started out as a simple outdoor venue, and grew organically until 1990, when its 120-tonne pyramidal roof proved the most innovative and successful solution to the island's new noise regulations. This set *Es Paradis* up for a consistently successful decade, with water parties (when the whole dancefloor is flooded) and Clockwork Orange club nights ensuring that the place was consistently packed. However, in recent years the club has suffered due to the popularity of the transformed *Eden* over the road, although R&B and soulful music nights fare well, including appearances by the UK's Twice as Nice crew.

▲ES PARADIS

Privilege

Ibiza–Sant Antoni road, km 6 ⓦwww.
privilege.es. May–Sept. See map p.94.
Listed in *The Guinness Book of
Records* as the world's largest
club (10,000 capacity), *Privilege*
is also home to Ibiza's biggest
night, Manumission. Hype aside,
the right night at this vast club
is quite an experience. As you
enter, the sheer scale of the
venue becomes apparent, with
a huge main dancefloor before
you, and the DJ plinth above the
club's swimming pool. On the
right are two separate areas: the
legendary *Coco Loco* zone where
DJs spin alternative sounds, and
a back room that becomes the
Music Box for Manumission,
showcasing live acts – expect
anything from trash electro to
hip hop (Goldie Lookin' Chain
played here in 2004). There are
fourteen bars scattered around,
two VIP zones on the upper
levels, while a vast, metal-framed
open-air dome forms the club's
alfresco chillout zone. There's
even a DJ in the toilets.

Formerly called *Ku*, for ten
years this was probably the
most beautiful, extravagant and
luxurious club in Europe. There
were huge terraces planted with
pine and palm trees, numerous
dancefloors and phenomenal
sound and light systems (the
laser shows could be seen in
Valencia), a swimming pool and
a top-class restaurant. Cocaine
spoons and champagne cocktails
were *de rigueur*, and there was
no shortage of celebrities:
Freddie Mercury sang Barcelona
here with Montserrat Caballé;
James Brown performed
here; and Grace Jones danced
naked in the rain here during
a thunderstorm. But laws
necessitating the construction
of a roof precipitated serious
financial problems by the 1990s,
and some would say destroyed
Ku's unique atmosphere. The
club also suffered badly from
under-investment, and was
eclipsed by the glamour of
Pacha and the innovation at
Amnesia. It wasn't until the
creative impetous and party
fever generated by the arrival
of Manumission in 1994 that
the club – renamed *Privilege*
the following year – started to
turn things around. The 2003
and 2004 seasons had some real
highlights, with Manumission
and Balearic People filling the
venue, however on most other
nights, even in peak season, the
vast hanger-like space can be
very quiet.

Summun

c/Cala de Bou, Sant Antoni bay.
June–Sept. In Sant Antoni bay,
3km west of the Egg, *Summun* is
a well-established comparatively
small (600 capacity) venue,
hosting a diverse selection of
nights, from R&B to eighties
pop crooners. Upstairs there's
a bar and a small rear terrace,
while the main body of
the club is in the basement.
Summun's bizarre decor is pretty
startling – walls painted with
swirling images of pastel angels
and gods reclining in alpine
scenery, plastercast gourds and
fruit hanging from the ceiling,
Roman columns and quarry
loads of marble. Entrance and
bar prices are reasonable by
Ibiza standards.

The south

Southern Ibiza is wildly beautiful and physically diverse, encompassing the island's highest peak, Sa Talaiassa, the shimmering Salines saltpans and drowsy one-horse villages, as well as a craggy coast staked with defence towers. The coastline is lapped by warm pellucid waters and endowed with more than a dozen beautiful beaches. The region has only three resorts – the quiet bays of Cala Vedella and Cala Tarida in the west, and big, brash Platja d'en Bossa in the extreme east; the rest of the shore is more or less pristine. Inland, the rolling, forested countryside is dotted with small attractive villages. There are also some very happening bars in the south, plus some great dining options, from simple shoreside chiringuitos to swanky country restaurants.

Sant Josep

Bus #8 from Ibiza Town, Mon–Sat 5 daily, Sun 2 daily; 20 min. Bus #8 from Sant Antoni, Mon–Sat 5 daily, Sun 2 daily; 15 min. Buses #42 & #26 from Ibiza Town (destination Cala Vedella) May–Oct, 6–9 daily; 20min.

Pretty, prosperous and easy-going Sant Josep has a delightful setting, 200m above sea level in a valley overlooked by the green, forested slopes of Sa Talaiassa. The village itself is of no great size, but it is the main settlement in the region.

There's a tidy, trim self-confidence here, best illustrated along the attractive, pint-sized high street, and just to the west around the exquisite little central plaza, where the Moorish-style tiled benches

▼ESGLÉSIA DE SANT JOSEP

Transport

Getting around the south is easy with your own vehicle, as there's a decent **road network** and plenty of signposts. **Buses** run along the main highway between Sant Antoni and Ibiza Town via Sant Josep, and there are also services to some beaches (indicated in the text).

are shaded by pines. From this plaza you have an excellent view across the main road to the imposing, whitewashed **Església de Sant Josep**, dating from 1726. The church has a superb three-storey facade, with a triple-arched porch that extends out from the main body of the building. It's only open for Mass, but if you do get to take a look at the capacious, delightfully cool interior, check out the wooden pulpit painted with scenes from the life of Christ, a reproduction of the eighteenth-century piece destroyed when the church's interior was gutted in the Spanish Civil War.

▲ESGLÉSIA DE SANT AGUSTÍ

Sant Agustí

About three kilometres north of Sant Josep, the pretty hilltop village of Sant Agustí is so tranquil that all signs of life seem to have been frazzled by the Mediterranean sun. Grouped around the fortified church at the heart of the settlement are a clump of old farmhouses, one of which has been beautifully converted into the *Can Berri Vell* restaurant (see p.141); there's also a village bar, a solitary store and an ancient stone defence tower where the locals once

hid from pirates. Captivating views across the hilly interior of the island and down to the southwest coast can be seen from the little plaza next to the landmark **Església de Sant Agustí**, completed in the early nineteenth century. Designed by the Spanish architect Pedro Criollez, this simple rectangular structure has a stark, whitewashed facade, but lacks the typical frontal porch of most Ibizan churches.

Sa Talaiassa

Towering above southern Ibiza, the 475-metre peak of Sa Talaiassa is the highest point in the Pitiuses. It's reachable either by an hour-long waymarked hike from Sant Josep, or dirt track (also signposted) that turns off the road to Cala Carbó, 2km west of Sant Josep. Thickly wooded with aleppo and Italian stone pines, the summit offers exceptional views of southern Ibiza from gaps between the trees. You should easily be able to pick out the humpback cliffs of Jondal and Falcó, the Salines saltpans and plateau-like Formentera – and on very clear days, the mountains of the Dénia peninsula in mainland Spain, some 50km distant. It's wonderfully peaceful here, the silence broken only by the buzz of cicadas and hum of a number of television antennae. In the 1960s, the summit was the scene of legendary full-moon parties staged by the hippy population.

Cala Tarida

Bus #5 from Sant Antoni, May–Oct 8 daily; 30min. Bus #38 from Ibiza Town May–Oct 5 daily; 35min. A wide arc of golden sand broken by two small rocky outcrops, Cala Tarida is where you'll find one of Ibiza's more appealing

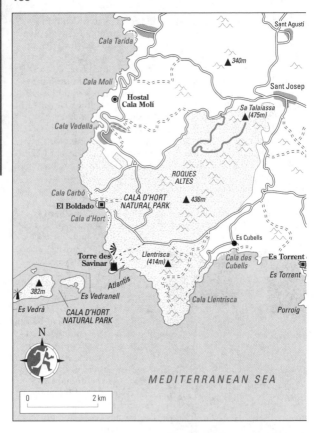

resorts, a small, family-oriented collection of low-rise hotels surrounding a pretty bay. In high season, the beach gets very busy with German and Spanish holidaymakers, and you'll have to pick your way through rows of umbrellas and sunbeds for a swim. There are plenty of fairly unexciting bars and restaurants to choose from; the best seafood is served at the expensive *Cas Mila*.

Cala Molí

Two kilometres south of Cala Tarida, the serpentine coast road dips down to Cala Molí,

▼CALA MOLÍ

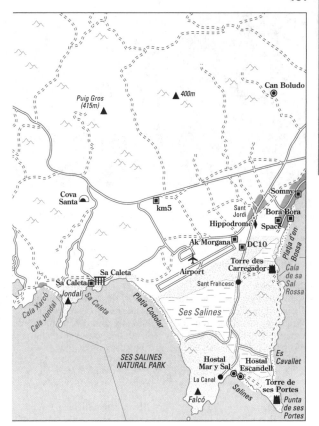

a fine beach at the foot of a seasonal riverbed. Steep cliffs envelop the pebbly cove, which is undeveloped except for the *Restaurante Cala Molí*, an eyesore which sells snacks and has a big swimming pool. The bay's sheltered, deep-green waters are very inviting, and, if you swim across to the cove's southern cliff, you can also explore a small cave. Cala Molí never seems to get too busy, probably because it's not served by buses – if you can get here independently, you'll find it's perfect for a chilled-out day by the sea.

Cala Vedella

Buses #26 & #42 from Ibiza Town, May–Oct 3 daily; 35–50min.
Continuing south from Cala Molí, the precipitous, shady road twists through the coastal pines for 3km, passing luxury holiday homes, before emerging above the long, narrow-mouthed inlet that harbours Cala Vedella. One of Ibiza's smallest and most attractive resorts, its profusion of good-quality villas and well-spaced, low-rise hotels are separated into two main developments dotted around the low hills framing the bay. The

▲CALA VEDELLA

sheltered, sandy beach is ideal for families, with calm, very shallow water and a collection of snack bars and restaurants backing onto the sands.

Cala Carbó

A tiny, tranquil cove-bay, Cala Carbó, 4km south of Cala Vedella, gets its name from the Catalan word for coal, which was unloaded here until the 1960s. There's a lovely little sand and pebble beach, which never seems to get too packed, backed by low sandstone cliffs, and tempting, calm sea; the mossy, rounded boulders offshore lend the water a deep jade tone. Snorkelling is good off the southern shore up to the rocky point at the mouth of the cove, where colourful wrasse and large schools of mirror fish are common. There are two seafood restaurants at the back of the bay.

Cala d'Hort

Bus #42 from Ibiza Town, May–Oct Mon–Fri 3 daily; 40min. The bus stops on the main road 800m above the beach. Cala d'Hort, 4km south of Cala Carbó, is an expansive beach of coarse sand and pebbles with one of the most spectacular settings in the Balearics. Directly opposite is

the startling, vertiginous rock-island of Es Vedrà (see below), while the beach is backed by the steep forested hillsides of the Roques Altes peaks, part of the beautiful **Cala d'Hort Natural Park**. There's a wonderfully isolated feel here, and the remote location, wedged into Ibiza's southwest corner, ensures that things never get too busy.

There are three good fish restaurants by the shore – the best is *El Boldado* on the northern lip of the bay (see p.141).

If you fancy sticking around in Cala d'Hort, try asking at the *El Carmen* restaurant if there's a room for rent.

Es Vedrà

Rising from the sea like the craggy crest of a semi-submerged volcano, the limestone outcrop of Es Vedrà is one of the most startling sights in the western Mediterranean. Despite its height (378m), it is only visible once you get within a few kilometres of Cala d'Hort. Legends surround the much-photographed rock, and it's said to be the island of the sirens (the sea-nymphs who tried to lure Odysseus from his ship in Homer's epic), as well as the holy isle of the Carthaginian love and fertility goddess, Tanit. A reclusive Carmelite priest, Father Palau i Quer, reported seeing visions of the Virgin Mary and satanic rituals here in the nineteenth century. Sailors and scuba divers have reported compasses swinging wildly and gauges malfunctioning as they approach the island, and there have been innumerable reports of UFO sightings.

These days, Es Vedrà is inhabited only by wild goats, a unique sub-species of the Ibizan wall lizard and a small colony of the endangered Eleanor's falcon. You can get to the island from Cala d'Hort by renting a four-metre boat, which will carry four, from Bruno's hut (☎607 147 155; €60 per hour) behind the beach; as the boat's engine has just 10HP a skipper's licence is not necessary. Vedrà has no beaches, however, and there's little to see, bar scrub bush and a lizard or two – even the goats usually prove elusive.

Torre des Savinar and Atlantis

Two kilometres along the exhilaratingly scenic road from Cala d'Hort to Es Cubells a right-hand turnoff leads to Torre des Savinar, a defence tower built in 1763 – it's also known (and signposted) as Torre d'en Pirata. The dirt track ends after 500m, where there's a small roundabout and parking area. From here it's a ten-minute walk to the coastal cliffs, where there's an amazing view over the sea to Es Vedrà, particularly at sunset.

From the tower itself there are even better vistas over Vedrà's sister island **Es Vedranell**, which resembles a sleeping dragon with its snout and spiky backbone protruding from the water.

Directly below the Torre des Savinar you can make out the outline of **Atlantis**, an ancient shoreside quarry some 200m down. To get there, retrace your steps to the mini-roundabout and take another path that sets

PLACES The south

▼ES VEDRÀ

off to the right (east); you'll quickly reach the clifftop trailhead from where Atlantis is a thirty-minute hike away. The very steep, well-trodden path is easy to follow; it flattens out after fifteen minutes beside a small **cave**, where there's a beautiful etched image of a Buddha, said to have been drawn by a Japanese traveller.

▲CALA LLENTRISCA

From the cave, you have to plough your way through sand dunes, but as you near the shore, the hewn forms of the ancient quarry – set at oblique angles from the bedrock – become clear. The stone here was used in the construction of Ibiza Town's magnificent walls.

Between the rock outcrops, shimmering indigo- and emerald-tinged pools of trapped seawater add an ethereal dimension to the scene. Much of the stone has been carved by hippies with mystic imagery – blunt-nosed faces resembling Maya gods, swirling abstract doodles and graffiti – while blocks of stone hang suspended by wires from the rock face. At the edge of the promontory there's a wonderful, partly painted carving of a Cleopatra-like oriental queen. Bring plenty of water and sun cream if you're heading for Atlantis as there's no shade.

Es Cubells

Bus #42 from Ibiza Town, May–Oct Mon–Fri 3 daily; 30min. South of Sant Josep, a signposted road weaves around the eastern flank of Sa Talaiassa, past terraces of orange and olive trees, to the southern coast and the tiny cliffside village of Es Cubells. The settlement owes its place on the map to Father Palau i Quer, a Carmelite priest who saw visions of the Virgin Mary in nearby Es Vedrà in the 1850s, and who persuaded the Vatican to construct a chapel here in 1855 for the local farmers and fishermen. Magnificently positioned above the Mediterranean, the simple whitewashed sandstone church is the focal point of the hamlet. Adjoining the church, *Bar Llumbi* is an inexpensive bar-restaurant. (May–Oct, closed Mon).

Cala des Cubells

Signposted from Es Cubells' church, the minuscule Cala des Cubells beach lies 1km from the village, via a couple of hairpin turns. It's one of Ibiza's least-visited spots, consisting of a slender strip of grey, tide-polished stones, with a few sunbeds and umbrellas and a somewhat overpriced restaurant, *Ses Boques*. If you're looking for an isolated place to get an all-over tan, head to the left past a strip of fishing huts, where three tiny, untouched stony beaches lie below grey, crumbling cliffs.

Cala Llentrisca

Southwest of Es Cubells, the road hugs the eastern slopes of the Llentrisca headland, descending for 3km past luxurious modern villas towards the lovely, unspoilt cove of Cala Llentrisca, cut off from the rest of the island by soaring pine-clad slopes. You'll need your own transport to get here; park beside the final villa at the end of the road and walk the last five minutes. Bear in mind that there's very little shade, and nothing on the pebbly shoreline except a row of seldom-used fishing huts, with a yacht or two often moored in the translucent waters.

Es Torrent

A small, sandy cove beach at the foot of a dry riverbed, Es Torrent lies 7km south of Sant Josep. To get here, take the road to Es Cubells, and follow the signposted turn-off that winds down towards the Porroig promontory. Es Torrent's waters are shallow and invitingly turquoise, and offer decent snorkelling around the cliffs at the edge of the bay. Though the beach is lovely, many people come here just for the expensive seafood restaurant, *Es Torrent* (see p.142).

Cala Xarcó

From Es Torrent, having looped around the Porroig peninsula, dotted with luxury villas, you can follow a dirt track that continues northeast for 400m to Cala Xarcó, a quiet strip of sand that only Ibizans and the odd yachtie seem to have stumbled upon. The coastal sabina pines here offer a little shade. There's also a sunbed or two for rent, and the superb (but very pricey) *Restaurant Es Xarcu*, which specializes in seafood.

Cala Jondal

The broad pebble beach of Cala Jondal lies between the promontories of Porroig and Jondal some 9km southeast of Sant Josep. A stony seashore at the base of terraces planted with fruit trees, Jondal's kilometre-long strip of smooth rounded stones and patches of imported sand doesn't make one of the island's very finest swimming spots, but there's always some space here and you should have no problem getting a sunbed and shade. There are some good beachside restaurants including *Yemaná* and *Tropicana* (which also serves excellent fresh fruit juices), and a massage tent (€25 per hour session) is located close to the centre of the beach. If you're coming from Xarcó, Cala Jondal is a couple of minutes' scramble over the cliff behind *Restaurant Es Xarcu*, or you can also drive via a precipitous dirt road from the beach; after 200m, take the first right beside some walled villas.

▼ CALA JONDAL

PLACES The south

Sa Caleta

Bus #42 from Ibiza Town, May–Oct Mon–Fri 3 daily; 20min. Four kilometres around the coast from Cala Jondal lie the **ruins** of Sa Caleta, the first Phoenician settlement in Ibiza. Established around 650 BC on a low promontory beside a tiny natural harbour, the small site was only occupied for about fifty years, before the Phoenicians moved to the site of what is now Ibiza Town. Today, a high metal fence surrounds the foundations of the village, once home to several hundred people, who lived by fishing, hunting and farming wheat as well as smelting iron for tools and weapons. The ruins are visually unimpressive, but the site is a peaceful place to visit, with expansive views over an azure sea towards Platja Codolar and Cap des Falcó.

Just west of the site are Sa Caleta's **beaches**, three tiny adjoining bays sometimes labelled as "Bol Nou" on maps. The first bay, a hundred-metre strip of coarse golden sand, is the busiest spot, and very popular with Ibizan families at weekends – there are some sunbeds and umbrellas to rent here in summer, excellent swimming and snorkelling, and the good, reasonably priced *Restaurante Sa Caleta* (see p.142). The other two bays, both secluded and pebbly, are to the west of the sandy bay, via a path that winds along the shore below Sa Caleta's low sandstone cliffs.

Platja Codolar

East of Sa Caleta, a road runs parallel to the ochre-coloured coastal cliffs, heading towards the airport and Sant Jordi. One kilometre along, there's a turn-off for Platja Codolar, a sweeping pebble beach that stretches for over 3km southeast, running close to the airport runway and skirting the fringes of the Salines saltpans. Even at the height of summer, there are rarely more than a dozen or so (mainly nude) swimmers and sunbathers here, and the place would be very peaceful were it not for the regular interruption of jet engines revving up on the runway or screaming overhead. It's also possible to get to the opposite end of Platja Codolar via the main road to Salines beach; turn off at km 3.6 and

▼SA CALETA

Platja d'en Bossa hike

It's possible to hike from Platja d'en Bossa to Es Cavallet along an easy-to-follow shady path that trails the coastline, passing rocky coves and through pine forests. From the extreme southernmost part of Platja d'en Bossa beach head to the six-teenth-century **Torre des Carregador**, a defence tower just above the beach, and continue to the south. The hike takes about an hour and doesn't stray more than 50m or so from the sea. There are no refreshments along the way.

follow the signposts for the *Cap des Falcó* restaurant.

Sant Jordi

Buses #10, #11, #26 & #42 from Ibiza Town 23–41 daily; 15min. Dismal-looking and traffic-choked, the small settlement of Sant Jordi is trapped in a kind of no-man's-land between Ibiza Town and the beaches to the south. Almost lost in the featureless suburban sprawl is the main point of interest, the **Església de Sant Jordi**, Ibiza's most fortress-like church, just east of the highway. With mighty angled walls gashed with embrasures and topped with full battlements – all security measures to keep out pirates – it's well worth a visit. Inside, the austerity of the gingham-tiled floor and simple wooden benches seem at odds with the gaudy modern altarpiece, installed in 1990.

The only other reason to visit Sant Jordi is for the very popular Saturday **market** (9am–2pm), actually more of a car boot sale, held in the dustbowl of the **hippodrome**, a former horse-and-buggy race track. It's Ibiza's most quirky affair, far less commercialized than the hippy markets, with a good selection of junk jewellery, trashy clothes, secondhand books and furniture.

Platja d'en Bossa

Bus #14 from Ibiza Town, May–Oct every 30min, plus hourly nightbuses; Nov–April hourly; 15min. A kilometre east of Sant Jordi,

and merging into Figueretes to the north (see p.64), the conventional, *costa*-style resort of Platja d'en Bossa is stretched out along the island's longest beach – a ruler-straight, three-kilometre-long strip of wonderfully fine, pale sand. Lining the beach are a gap-toothed row of hotel blocks, many abruptly thrown up in the later Franco years and others still in various stages of construction; behind these lies a secondary strip of cafés, touristy restaurants, German bierkellers, British pubs, car-rental outlets and minimarkets filled with plastic dolphins, lilos and sun creams. Though Platja d'en Bossa is predominantly a family resort, it's also famous for the bombastic antics at the beachside club-bar *Bora Bora* (see p.143).

Despite the tourist tat, Platja d'en Bossa is increasingly popular as a base for savvy, older clubbers who have tired of the San An scene and stay here to take advantage of the location – a few kilometres equidistant from Ibiza Town and the sands at Salines. Its main drawback is the lack of decent restaurants, most of which serve bland "international" fare.

Aguamar

May–Oct 10am–6pm. €16, children over 2 years €8. Bus #14 from Ibiza Town, every 30min; 15min. With a great selection of slides and a vast central swimming pool area suitable for all ages, this water park is a lot of fun. It's also well managed, with attendants on standby to ensure safety requirements

are enforced. It does get very busy in July and August, when you'll have to queue for a while for the best rides. There are several snack bars and picnic areas, though you have to pay extra to use sunbeds and lockers.

Salines beach

Bus #11 from Ibiza Town, May–Oct 10 daily; Nov–April 4 daily; 20min. A beautiful kilometre-long strip of powdery pale sand backed by pines and dunes, Salines beach is Ibiza's most fashionable place to pose. The sands are interspersed with rocky patches, and beach bars dot the shoreline, which changes from a family-friendly, bucket-and-spade environment close to the *Guaraná* café in the north into the island's premier navel-gazing spot around the über-hip café *Sa Trinxa* in the south, where you can sunbathe nude. Beyond *Sa Trinxa* are a succession of tiny sandy coves, enveloped by unusual rock formations – some were once quarried centuries ago, while more recently, talented sculptors have carved images into the coastal stone, including a Medusa-like figure and a fang-baring dragon wearing a Maya-style headdress. These mini-beaches tend to get grabbed fairly early in the day

▼SALINES BEACH

▲ES CAVALLET

and jealously guarded as private bays by dedicated – and pretty territorial – sunbathers. Beyond the coves, the sands give way to a slender rocky promontory, topped at its end by the **Torre de ses Portes** defence tower.

Es Cavallet

Es Cavallet is a stunning beach, where Franco's Guardia Civil fought a futile battle against nudism for years, arresting hundreds of naked hippies before the kilometre-long stretch of sand was finally designated Ibiza's first naturist shore in 1978. The northern end of the beach, close to *La Escollera* restaurant (see p.142) and the car park, attracts a mixed bunch of families and couples, but the southern half of the beach – and the nicest stretch – is almost exclusively gay, centred around the superb *Chiringay* bar-café (see p.141).

Punta de ses Portes

A fifteen-minute walk south from Es Cavallet beach is Ibiza's most southerly point, Punta de ses Portes, a lonely, rocky spot, often lashed by winds and waves. Above the swirling currents and a handful of surf-battered

Salines saltpans

Ibiza's spectacular saltpans, which stretch across 435 hectares in the south of the island, were the island's only reliable source of wealth for more than 2000 years. The Phoenicians first developed the land and while Roman, Vandal and Visigoth invaders continued to maintain the saltpans, it was the Moors, experts at hydraulic technology, who developed the system of sluice gates, mini-windmills and water channels that's still in use today. Each May approximately 2500 cubic metres of seawater is left to evaporate, forming a ten-centimetre crust of pinky-white powder that is scooped up and amassed in huge salt hills. Around 70,000 tonnes of salt are exported annually; the finest quality is shipped to Norway for salting cod, and the rest to Scotland for salting roads in winter.

As well as producing salt, the pans (part of a wetland reserve) are also an important habitat for **birds**, being one of the first points of call on the migratory route from Africa. Storks, herons and flamingoes stop to rest and refuel, as well as over 200 species in permanent residence, from osprey and black-necked grebe to Kentish plover. A visitor centre has been long planned next to the church in Sant Francesc, but until it opens, you're best viewing the pans at sunset from the Sant Jordi–La Canal road, around the km 3 marker; beware clouds of mosquitoes at dusk and dawn, especially in September.

fishing huts is a two-storey, sixteenth-century defence tower, **Torre de ses Portes**, which commands superb views of the chain of tiny islands that reach out to Formentera. One of these, Illa des Penjats (Island of the Hanged), was used for executions until the early twentieth century; another, Illa des Porcs (Pig Island), was once a pig smugglers' stronghold. Both islands are topped by the lighthouses that guide ships and ferries through the treacherous Es Freus channel between Ibiza and Formentera.

Hotels

Hostal Cala Molí

1km south of Cala Molí ☎971 806 002, ⊛www.calamoli.com. May–Oct. High in the hills with great sunset vistas, this small, welcoming hotel has attractive, good-value accommodation decorated with textile wall-hangings; all rooms overlook the sea and some come with their own lounge (€95–104). There's a small pool, a restaurant and breakfast is included. €76–88.

Hotel Los Jardins de Palerm

Sant Josep ☎971 800 318, ⊛www.jardinsdepalerm.com. Small, peacefully situated luxury hotel, a short walk away from the village of Sant Josep. The stylish rooms and suites (the latter starting at €189) have air con and cable TV; there's a lush garden, a decent bar and restaurant, and a beautiful pool. Continental breakfast is included. €155–176.

Pensions

Hostal Mar y Sal

Salines beach ☎971 396 584, ☎971 395 453. For beach-lovers on a budget this basic *hostal*, just behind Salines beach, is ideal. The smallish rooms have private showers and some have balconies with views of the sand dunes; there's also a good bar/restaurant downstairs. €42.

Hostal Pepita Escandell

Salines beach ☎971 396 583. May–Oct. Tiny, very friendly place at the northern end of Salines beach with tidy, basic rooms; some have private bathrooms. There's a communal kitchen and tranquil garden. €38.

▼SA TRINXA

Cafés

Chiringay

Es Cavallet beach. April–Oct daily
10am–8pm. Celebrated beachfront
bar-restaurant on Ibiza's main gay
beach with a great selection of
juices, fruit smoothies and healthy
food, as well as a resident masseur.
Spread over wooden decks, all
the tables have sea views.

▲CAN BERRI VELL

Sa Trinxa

Salines beach ⊕ www.satrinxa
.com. Daily: April–Oct 11am–10pm; Nov–
March 11am–7pm. The definitive
Ibizan *chiringuito*, set at the
southern end of the hippest beach
on the island. Emotive, soulful
sounds from resident DJ Jonathan
Grey and guests, and a bevy
of Balearic wildlife, including
clubberati, models, party freaks
and Euro slackers, to observe.
Meals served, but the *bocadillos* are
some of the priciest in Ibiza.

Restaurants

Can Berri Vell

Plaça Major, Sant Agustí ⊕ 971
344 321. 12.30–3.30pm & 8pm–
midnight: Sept–June Thurs–Sat;
July & Aug daily. This restaurant
has a terrific setting inside
a historic Ibizan *casament*
(farmhouse) with a warren
of rooms and a large dining
terrace with views over
the village church and the
southern hills. There's a simple
menu, majoring in grilled
meats; expect to pay about
€30 per person including
drinks.

Can Boludo

Camí del Cementeri
Nou ⊕ 971 391 883
Jan & March–Dec
daily 9pm–
midnight. Funky
Argentinian-
owned
restaurant, set
in a converted
country house,
with a rustic
interior and
elevated terrace
overlooking
the island. The
menu includes
prime cuts of
Argentinian steak, fish, pasta
and unusual South American
desserts – expect to pay around
€35 per person. *Can Boludo* is
reached via a side road marked
"Cementeri Nou" that heads
north off the Ronda E-20 Ibiza
Town outer ring road.

El Boldado

Cala d'Hort ⊕ 626 494 537 (mobile).
Daily 1–4pm & 7.30–10.30pm.
Overlooking Es Vedrà, this
seafood restaurant boasts a
stunning location, particularly at
sunset. The menu offers superb
paella (€27 for two), *arroz
marinera* and plenty of excellent
grilled fish (from €14), though
nothing for dessert except ice
cream. You can drive to *El
Boldado* via a signposted side
road just northwest of Cala

d'Hort, or it's a five-minute walk west of the same beach, past the fishermen's huts.

El Destino

c/Atalaya 15, Sant Josep ☎971 800 341. Mon–Sat 7.30pm–midnight. Set off Sant Josep's village plaza, this excellent little restaurant has a healthy, inexpensive menu that includes tapas and plenty of choice for vegetarians. There's a small pavement terrace and a comfortable dining room. Book ahead on summer nights.

Es Torrent

Es Torrent beach ☎971 187 402. May–Oct daily 1–10pm. Deceptively simple-looking place with a wonderful shoreside setting, serving excellent, but expensive, grilled and baked fish, lobster and seafood. As there's no menu, the Ibizan proprietor Xicu guides you through the daily specials and makes recommendations. Popular with a yachtie crowd.

La Escollera

Es Cavallet beach ☎971 396 572. May–Oct daily 1pm–12.30am; Nov–April 1–5.30pm. Very enjoyable restaurant, with sweeping views of Es Cavallet's sandy beach

and Formentera. There's a huge outdoor terrace by the sea and a capacious interior. Signature dishes include *zarzuela* (fish and seafood casserole) and paella (€26 for two), though there are meat options including steaks and country-style chicken.

Sa Caleta

Sa Caleta beach ☎971 187 095. May–Oct noon–midnight; Nov–April noon–7pm. Fine, fairly expensive seafood restaurant, just behind this popular cove beach. Fish is grilled, baked or served in *salsa verde*; there's also good paella and great apple tart. For a memorable finish order the house special, Sa Caleta coffee, which is prepared at your table and includes a generous dose of brandy and lemon and orange peel.

Bars

AK Morgana

Sant Jordi–airport road, km 1. Daily June–Sept 11pm–4am. Striking bar, set in a two-storey villa, with a large terrace garden and an internal dancefloor. Like *km 5*, *Morgana* regularly has problems with its dance licence, but on a

▼BORA BORA

busy night this is a great place to socialize with a fashionable Ibizan crowd.

Bar Can Bernat Vinye

Sant Josep. Daily 7am–midnight. Unpretentious locals' local in Sant Josep village, serving inexpensive tapas and snacks, where Spanish is a second language to Eivissenc. In summer, tables spill onto the delightful plaza outside; the conversation usually centres on rainfall, lucrative house rentals and the strange ways of *giris* (tourists).

Bora Bora

Platja d'en Bossa. May–Sept daily noon–midnight. Beach rave bar-club set on Platja d'en Bossa's golden sands that for years flouted Ibiza's strict noise regulations, unleashing pounding house to a cast of thousands in high season. The authorities, however, closed the premises at the end of the 2004 season, so the bar's future was uncertain at the time of writing. If it reopens, you may find *Bora Bora* is not your cup of tea, but it's definitely one of the island's unique experiences. No door tax, no queues and reasonably priced drinks.

km 5

Ibiza Town–Sant Josep road, km 5.6. June–Sept daily 9pm–4am; Oct–May Wed, Fri & Sat 11pm–4am. Elegant, urbane bar-restaurant that draws an international crowd, set in a rustic nowhereland west of Ibiza Town, with a huge garden decked out with Moroccan tents and rugs for relaxed drinking and socializing. The food is great: free-range chicken, steaks and a good vegetarian selection. There are often live DJs too, though Ibiza's draconian licensing laws means that the dancefloor is periodically roped off.

Clubs

Space

Platja d'en Bossa ⊛www.space-ibiza.es. June–Oct. A vast (3000 capacity) cream-coloured structure just off Platja d'en Bossa beach, *Space* is essentially a day venue, kicking off after sunrise when the other clubs are closing (though there are also a few night events). This carry-on-clubbing scene, centred on the venue's legendary terrace, attracts a very hardcore crowd, and perhaps the most cosmopolitan mix in Ibiza, including Balearic-based clubbing folk, international party freaks and a big gay contingent. Since the start of the 1990s, Sundays here have been one of *the* most fashionable places to be seen, but the ever-increasing numbers have diluted the Ibizan character of the club somewhat, and now the Saturday session, which still has

▼SPACE

much more of a local flavour, has risen in popularity.

The club is divided into two main parts: a dark, cavernous, bunker-like interior, and a wonderful terrace graced with fine sandstone walls, greenery and a sweeping mahogany bar. The brushwood roof of the terrace will have a retractable glass ceiling installed for the 2005 season, which should enable the owners to keep it open until 6am. Other renovations have added two new upper-level areas: a chillout VIP balcony, and the *Caja Roja* (Red Box) – an intimate, alternative room that got off to a strong start in 2004 with Smokin' Jo and Tim Sheriden taking up Sunday residency. The massive main room of the club will also be steadily revamped over the next few years, though it's likely to remain dark and moody – an ideal setting for pounding, harder beats.

Somny

Platja d'en Bossa. June–Sept. This mid-sized club (800 capacity) emerged in 2004 after the partition of the tacky *Kiss discoteca*, long the haunt of wet T-shirt competitions and singalong holiday hits, resulted in two separate venues. *Somny* certainly looks the part, with very stylish lighting, seating and attractive bar zones, a roof terrace and an impressive sound system. However the odd night aside, the venue has yet to really establish its own identity. The Chilean-Anglo promoted *Arthrob* session is generally a good bet with a cosmopolitan crowd and quality house DJs, including Samir; guest turntablists have also included Berliners Tiefschwarz and Trevor Fung. Entrance and drinks prices are substantially cheaper than the other big clubs.

DC10

Sant Jordi–Salines road, km 1. June–Sept. One of *the* success stories of the last few years, this daytime club has a raw, unpretentious appeal completely different to the more corporate-minded venues. Forgoing commerce for pure party spirit, *DC10* has been dubbed "the new *Space*" by a multitude of Ibiza scenesters; at times, the atmosphere here can rival the old acid house days, as a euphoric international crowd of smiling faces dance in the sunshine. The Anglo-Italian Circo Loco ensemble started a Monday daytime slot with DJ Jo Mills and guests here in 2000, which was followed by some amazing sessions, including epic performances by Danny Tenaglia and Timo Mass. With assorted superstar DJs clamouring to get behind the turntables it's sure to be huge in the next few years.

The club is located in a rural corner of Ibiza, a stone's throw from the airport. The covered terrace, where all the action takes place, is little more than a wall around a paved floor, overlooked by the giant reeds of neighbouring fields. Adjoining the terrace is a scruffy interior room, with harder, more progressive sounds, that rarely gets busy.

▲DC10

Formentera

Tranquil, easy-going Formentera could hardly be more of a contrast to Ibiza. The island is very flat, consisting of two shelf-like plateaux connected by a narrow central isthmus, and has a population of just 7000. Most visitors are drawn here by the languid pace of life, as well as some of the longest, whitest, cleanest and least-crowded beaches in Spain, surrounded by exceptionally clear water. This unhurried appeal belies a troubled past: the struggle of eking out a living from the saltpans and the sun-baked soil, combined with outbreaks of the plague and attacks by pirates, led Formentera to be completely abandoned in the late fourteenth century, only to be resettled in 1697. The island has just one resort, Es Pujols, a restrained, small-scale affair, with the pick of the beaches close by. Inland, the beautiful, if arid, countryside is a patchwork of golden wheatfields, vines, carob and fig trees, divided by old dry-stone walls. Of the three villages, the central, diminutive capital, Sant Francesc Xavier is the most interesting, and equally captivating are the island's extremes, where you'll find lonely lighthouses, surrounded by stunning coastal scenery.

La Savina

Set in a small natural harbour in the northwest corner of the island, small, orderly La Savina is likely to be your first view of Formentera, as all ferries from Ibiza dock here. Never more than a minor settlement for the export of salt and planks of sabina pine (from which it takes its name), it's still a sleepy place today when the ferry

▼MARINA, LA SAVINA

Transport

Most visitors choose to get around Formentera independently and renting transport is easy (see p.167). There's a good network of Green Route cycle paths (leaflets are available from the tourist office, see p.148; for bike rental see p.168). The island also has a pretty reasonable **bus** network, with daily services operating a loop around the main settlements of La Savina, Es Pujols, Sant Ferran and Sant Francesc every two hours or so between May and October, plus buses to La Mola and Platja Illetes. Services are much reduced for the rest of the year.

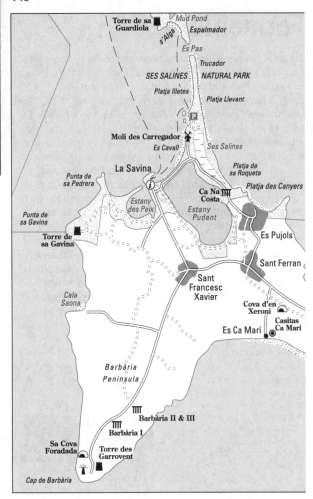

Torre de sa
Guardiola
Mud Pond
s'Alga
Espalmador

Es Pas

Trucador

SES SALINES   NATURAL PARK

Platja Illetes

Platja Llevant

Molí des Carregador
Es Cavall   Ses Salines

La Savina

Platja de
sa Roqueta

Punta de
sa Pedrera

Ca Na
Costa

Platja des Canyers

Punta de
sa Gavina

Estany
des Peix

Estany
Pudent

Es Pujols

Torre de
sa Gavina

Sant Ferran

Cala
Saona

Sant
Francesc
Xavier

Cova d'en
Xeroni

Casitas
Ca Marí

Es Ca Marí

Barbària
Peninsula

Barbària II & III

Barbària I

Sa Cova
Foradada

Torre des
Garrovent

Cap de Barbària

traffic subsides. While not that
absorbing, the modern harbour
is pleasant enough, and the
souvenir shops and cafés are
perfectly placed if you need
to while away an hour or so
before your ferry departs. Most
of the eateries offer broadly
similar menus, but the stylish
Aigua (see p.160) has the best
food and most comfortable
surroundings.

Estany Pudent and Estany des Peix

Buses on the La Savina–La Mola
highway pass within 300m of both
lakes. Heading southeast out
of La Savina, the island's main
highway passes a sprawl of
roadside warehouses that almost
obscure Formentera's two salt
lakes, the island's main wetland
habitats. On the left, Estany
Pudent, or "Stinking Pond", is

the larger of the two, an oval expanse that smells better now that an irrigation channel has been opened to allow seawater in, though a rotten aroma sometimes hangs in the air on still days. Ringed by scrub bush and an unsightly jumble of bungalows, it's not exactly pretty, but is popular amongst birdwatchers, who come to see herons and egrets, black-necked grebes, warblers and even the odd flamingo. Dirt tracks run around the entire lake; you can get to the shoreline via a left-hand turn-off 500m along the main highway from La Savina, which passes through a small patch of saltpans.

Smaller Estany des Peix, to the right of the highway via a turn-off 1km south of La Savina, has a narrow mouth to the sea,

Arrival and information

Several companies run **ferries** and **hydrofoils** between Ibiza Town and La Savina (July–Sept 12–16 daily; Nov–March 5 daily; April–June & Oct 9–12 daily; 30–65min; €18–29 return). In addition, boat operators in most Ibiza resorts offer day trips to Formentera.

Just behind the harbour in La Savina, Formentera's only **tourist information** office (Mon–Fri 10am–2pm & 5–7pm; Sat 10am–2pm; ☎971 322 057; ⊛www. formentera.es) has a good stock of glossy leaflets covering the island's history, environment, hotels, beaches and Green Routes, and the staff are extremely helpful. For **accommodation** information, head next door to the Central de Reservas Formentera office (☎971 323 224, ⊛www.formenterareservations.com), which has an extensive list of apartments and houses for rent.

and its shallow waters act as an ideal nursery for young fish. The brackish lagoon is no more picturesque than its neighbour, and not as rich birding territory, but there are plenty of terns and ducks and you may encounter the odd wader. Endemic marine organisms found in the lake have also been found to have strong cancer-fighting qualities. After four years of successful clinical trials in the USA and several EU countries, an extract from a tunicate found in Estany des Peix will be marketed as Yondelis (ET-743), a treatment for tumours.

Sant Francesc Xavier

Bus from La Savina, May–Oct 14 daily; Nov–April 3 daily; 5min. Formentera's tiny capital, Sant Francesc Xavier, 2km southeast of La Savina, is a quiet little town with an attractive network of pretty, whitewashed streets.

It's not much of a social centre – though it does have a few bars – and Sant Francesc's residents have the reputation of being a somewhat sedate bunch. If you've arrived from the mainland or from Ibiza Town, you'll have to get used to very un-Spanish timekeeping here – eating before 10pm and drinking up shortly after 11pm.

Plaça de sa Constitució

The heart of Sant Francesc is the Plaça de sa Constitució, a fetching little square, with a few benches scattered between gnarled olive trunks and sickly-looking palm trees. Consecrated in 1726, the forbidding, fortified **Església de Sant Francesc Xavier** stands on the north side of the plaza, its stark plastered facade embellished only with a tiny window set high in the wall. Until the mid-nineteenth century cannons were mounted

▾CYCLISTS, ESTANY PUDENT

▲SANT FRANCESC XAVIER, PLAÇA DE SA CONSTITUCIÓ

on the building's flat roof as an extra line of defence against pirate attacks, an ever-present threat. Entering the church through the mighty main doors, strengthened with iron panelling, the sombre interior has a single barrel-vaulted nave, five tiny side chapels and a gaudy gold-plated altar. Beside the doorway, the large, alabaster baptismal font is its most curious feature, decorated with a crudely executed ox's head and weathered human faces. It's thought to date from Vandal times, but no one is quite sure who originally brought it here. Adjoining the church to the south is the unpretentious, blue-shuttered old government building, while on the opposite side of the square is its attractive modern replacement, the **Casa de sa Constitució**, built from local sandstone.

Sa Tanca Vell

c/Eivissa, 100m south of Plaça de sa Constitució. Sant Francesc's second chapel, the primitive fourteenth-century Sa Tanca Vell, is worth a quick visit. Barely 5m long by 2m high and topped with a simple barrel-vaulted roof, it was originally constructed in 1362 from rough sandstone blocks, and the partly ruined remains were rebuilt in 1697, when Formentera was resettled. Sa Tanca Vell must have been a horrendously claustrophobic place to take Mass or seek refuge from pirates, with just enough space for a congregation of a dozen or so. After the resettlement, it served as the island's only place of worship for thirty years, until the much larger Església de Sant Francesc Xavier was completed. Today, the building is fenced in and not open to the public, but you can get a clear enough view of the exterior through the protective railings.

Museu Etnològic

100m northwest of Plaça de sa Constitució on c/Sant Jaume. Mon–Sat 10am–1.30pm. Free. Sant Francesc's modest Museu Etnològic, situated above a little cultural centre, has a moderately interesting collection of highly polished old farming tools and fishing gear. There are also a few curious old photographs of the island, including one from the early twentieth century of a very muddy, desolate-looking Sant Francesc. Outside the museum is the tiny toy-town steam train that used to shunt the island's salt to the docks from the saltpans.

Cala Saona

South of Sant Francesc, an undulating, ruler-straight main road runs for 2.5km to a signposted branch road that veers west through rust-red fields of carob and fig, and small coppices of aleppo pine, to the appealing bay of Cala Saona, 3km from the junction. The only cove beach in Formentera (and a fairly busy spot in the summer), Cala Saona has temptingly turquoise water, and fine sand that extends 100m back from the coast to the big *Hotel Cala Saona*, the bay's only building.

There are some fine cliffside walking routes south of Cala Saona, along coastal paths that meander past sabina pines and sand dunes and offer plenty of quiet, shady spots for a picnic lunch. The sunset views from this section of the coast are stunning, with a

dramatic perspective over the Mediterranean to the sphinx-like contours of Es Vedrà and Es Vedranell, and to the soaring hills of southern Ibiza; on exceptionally clear days you can make out the jagged mountains around Dénia on the mainland.

Barbària peninsula ruins

Continuing south from the Cala Saona turn-off, the road gradually begins its ascent of Formentera's southern plateau, the sparsely populated Barbària peninsula. Along the route there are a collection of minor archeological sites, all signposted from the road. First are the fenced-off remnants of the 3800-year-old Bronze Age **Barbària II** which contained nine simple limestone buildings – bedrooms, workrooms, a kiln and animal quarters. It's beautifully located amidst small arid fields dotted with carob trees and dense patches of pine, which serve as prime habitats for birdlife, including flycatchers and the exotic, zebra-striped hoopoe.

The other sets of remains, **Barbària III** and **Barbària I**, also date from the Bronze Age. Barbària III's singularly

▾CALA SAONA

▲FAR DES BARBÀRIA

unremarkable buildings may have been animal pens while Barbària I consists of a three-metre-wide circular formation of upended stone blocks that may have represented a place of worship, but practically nothing is known about their significance.

Cap de Barbària

The southernmost point in the Pitiuses forms an eerily beautiful, almost lunar landscape. This isolated region, the Cap de Barbària, or "Barbary Cape", is named after the North African pirates who passed this way to plunder the Balearics. The bleak, sun-bleached landscape, dotted with tiny green patches of hardy rosemary and thyme, boasted a dense pine wood until the 1930s, when ruined emigrés, returning to a jobless Formentera during the American Depression, chopped down the trees to make charcoal.

At the end of the road a white-painted lighthouse, the **Far des Barbària**, stands above the swirling, cobalt-blue waters of the Mediterranean, and from here you are likely to spot gulls, shearwaters and peregrine falcons. If you pick your way 200m south of the lighthouse, you'll find a cave, **Sa Cova Foradada**, which is worth a quick look. You enter by lowering yourself into a small hole in the roof of the modest single chamber; once you're inside, you can edge your way to the mouth of the cave, almost 100m above the sea, for a stunning view of the Mediterranean.

Northeast of the lighthouse, it's a ten-minute walk over to **Torre des Garroveret**, a well-preserved, two-storey eighteenth-century tower. As Formentera's first line of defence against Barbary pirates, it would have been manned night and day in centuries past, but is no longer open. Formenterans claim that on exceptionally clear days it's possible to see the mountains of North Africa from here, despite the fact that they're 110km away.

Sant Ferran

Bus from La Savina, May–Oct 14 daily; Nov–April 3 daily; 10min. Strung out along a busy junction on the main La Savina–La Mola highway, Sant Ferran ("San Fernando" in Castilian), Formentera's second largest town, has an abundance of banks, bars, stores and restaurants. With its two main streets plagued by traffic noise and lined with unsteady-looking apartment blocks, your first impression of Sant Ferran may make you want to head straight out again. However, the most attractive part of town, hidden away a couple of streets northeast of the main highway, is well worth investigating, centred around the pleasantly austere village church, **Església de Sant Ferran**. The church was originally built close to the island's saltpans towards the end of the eighteenth century but poor construction methods and the unsuitability of the sandy terrain meant that the structure started to crumble; in 1883 it was taken down, and over the next six years reconstructed stone by stone in today's location. Uniquely in the Pitiuses, its simple sandstone facade, topped with a crude belfry, has not been plastered or whitewashed.

Opposite the church is a spacious, paved **plaza**, lined with seats and young palm trees. There's barely a soul to be seen here for most of the year, but during the summer months it becomes a meeting place for young Formenterans and holidaying teenagers. The more

mature can be found just down the road at the *Fonda Pepe* (see p.161) or eating at one of the string of restaurants south of the plaza.

Es Pujols

Bus from La Savina, May–Oct 14 daily; Nov–April 3 daily; 15min.
Formentera's only designated resort, Es Pujols, 2km north of Sant Ferran, is an attractive, small-scale affair, popular with young Germans and Italians. It's lively but not overtly boisterous, with a decent quota of bars and a small club. Curving off to the northwest, in front of the clump of hotels and apartment blocks, is the reason why virtually everyone is here: the **beach** – two crescents of fine white sand, separated by a low rocky coastal shelf and dotted with ramshackle fishing huts. The beautiful shallow, turquoise water here heats up to tropical temperatures by August, when it can get very crowded, with rows of sunbeds packing the sands. There's nothing much to see away from the beach, and most visitors spend the evening wandering along the promenade, selecting a seafront restaurant and browsing the market stalls.

▼ES PUJOLS

The summer bar scene is as lively as you'll get in Formentera, though the odd venue aside, the music is standard-issue Mediterranean holiday-mix tapes. It's not difficult to find the action, mostly centred on c/Espardell just off the promenade and in the streets behind. The hippest spots in town are probably the *Riamblu* and the revamped *Xueño* club next door (see p.162).

▼CA NA COSTA

Ca Na Costa

Bus from Es Pujols, May–Oct 5 daily; 2min. A kilometre northwest of Es Pujols, signposted just off the road to the Salines saltpans and overlooking the waters of Estany Pudent, is the fenced-off megalithic tomb of Ca Na Costa. This tiny but archeologically important site represents the earliest proof of human habitation in Formentera, consisting of a stone circle of upright limestone slabs, up to 2m high, surrounded by concentric circles of smaller stones. These stand adjacent to a mass grave, where the skeletons of eight men and two women have been found – one of the male specimens, at some 2m tall, is thought to have been a sufferer of gigantism. Archeologists have also unearthed flint tools here, not found anywhere else

in the Pitiuses, and ceramic fragments indicating that early Formenterans were trading with Mallorca, suggesting a relatively sophisticated early society with established trade routes.

Platja des Canyers and Platja de sa Roqueta

Bus from La Savina, May–Oct 7 daily; 10min. One kilometre north of Ca Na Costa along the road that skirts the east coast, a signposted turnoff on the right leads to two neighbouring sandy bays, Platja des Canyers and Platja de sa Roqueta – not amongst Formentera's most scenic beaches, but both offering good swimming in calm shallow water, and hosting kiosks selling refreshments.

Es Cavall and the Molí des Carregador

Just west of the saltpans, the slender, sandy beach of Es Cavall (sometimes called Cala Savina) has two excellent, though pricey *chiringuitos* – *Big Sur* and *Tiburón* – and great swimming, as well as some shade from the coastal pines. Just north of the beach, along a sandy track, there's a huge old windmill, Molí des Carregador, that used to pump seawater into the saltpans – it's now been converted into a mediocre but expensive seafood restaurant.

Trucador peninsula

A slender finger of low-lying land, the idyllic Trucador peninsula, extends north towards the island of Espalmador. Virtually the entire length of this sandy promontory, part of Ses Salines Natural Park, is blessed with exquisite beaches

Salines saltpans

Formentera's shimmering saltpans lie at the very top of the island. Though they haven't been in commercial use since 1984 (unlike their equivalent on Ibiza – see p.139), crystallization in the steely-blue pools continues nevertheless, with foam-like clusters of salt clinging to the fringes of the low stone walls that divide the pans.

As an extension to Estany Pudent and Estany des Peix, the saltpans form an important wetland zone, attracting gulls, terns, waders and flamingoes, the latter encouraged (or perhaps confused) by the presence of two dozen pink concrete impostors. The pans and surrounding coastal region of northern Formentera, as well as southern Ibiza and Espalmador, are included within a protected "natural park" where building is prohibited.

lapped by shallow waters.

From the Molí des Carregador windmill, a sandy track heads north through steep sand dunes, passing a turn-off on the right for a short track that twists around the tip of the saltpans eastwards to **Platja Llevant**, a glorious undeveloped beach that forms the east coast of the Trucador peninsula. This eye-dazzling stretch of white sand is also where you'll find the large, popular *Tango* beach restaurant.

Continuing northwards up the peninsula, the sandy track eventually ends beside a huge car park packed with hundreds of scooters and bicycles in high season. Just offshore are two small islets, **Pouet** and **Rodona**, that give this slim stretch of beach its name: **Platja Illetes**. The sands here are very popular with day-trippers from Ibiza in high season, when you can rent windsurfing equipment from a beachside hut.

You'll have to continue on foot if you want to explore the very narrow final section of the peninsula, barely 30m wide, bordered by blinding white powdery sand that never seems to get too busy. These back-to-back beaches are Formentera's very best, with astonishingly clear, turquoise-tinged water on both sides of the slim, sandy

finger of land. A kilometre from the car park, you reach the northerly tip of Formentera, **Es Pas**, or "The Crossing", partially connected to the island of Espalmador by a 300-metre sandbar. If the sea is not too choppy, you should be able to cross over without soaking your belongings.

Espalmador

A shelf-like island of dunes and sandstone rock, most people visit Espalmador for stunning **s'Alga beach**, with its dazzling, shallow water and fine arc of white sand. In summer, the sheltered bay bristles with yachts, and is a favoured destination for day-trippers from Ibiza (many of the Formentera-bound boat-trips from Ibiza stop here on their way to La Savina). Some visitors take time out to visit the **sulphurous mud pond** a few minutes' walk north of the beach – you'll probably have it to yourself if you visit early or late in the day. The entire crust of the four-hectare pool has dried out considerably in recent years because of declining rainfall, but, even in the height of summer, there are three or four small patches of softer mud that you can climb down to for a good writhe around in gooey bliss. The one monument, aptly named **Torre de sa Guardiola** ("Piggy-bank Tower") on the western flank of the island, is a two-storey eighteenth-century defence tower – with a slot-like opening on its flank – clearly visible from the decks of ferries heading to Ibiza.

at vaguely Santa Claus-like formations, it's not really worth the bother.

Platja de Migjorn

Vying with the Trucador beaches for status as Formentera's finest strip

▲MUD POND, ESPALMADOR

Cova d'en Xeroni

May–Oct 10am–2pm & 5–8pm. €3.50. Southeast of Sant Ferran, Formentera's main highway descends towards a central isthmus, only a couple of kilometres wide in places. Just off the highway at the 6km marker, there's a signposted turn-off for Cova d'en Xeroni, a large limestone cave consisting of a single, forty-metre-wide cavern, that was accidentally discovered in the 1970s when the owner of the land started drilling for a well. His son now conducts regular tours of the chamber's spiky crop of stalactites and stalagmites, though only in German, Italian, Spanish or Catalan. The tour has a certain kitsch appeal, as the owners have lit the cavern with 1970s disco lights, but unless you're interested in gawping

of sand, Platja de Migjorn ("Midday Beach") is a sublime six-kilometre swathe of pale sand washed by gleaming, azure water, extending along the entire south coast of Formentera's central strip. Most of it is more or less pristine, with development confined to the extremities – at the western end, **Es Ca Marí**, signposted 3km south of Sant Ferran, is a loose scattering of hotel blocks set back from the sand, while at the eastern end, Mar i Land comprises two large hotels (see p.157). To get to the best stretch of sand, turn south off the highway around the 8km marker, where a bumpy dirt track passes through wonderfully picturesque fields of wheat and fig trees separated by Formentera's characteristic dry-stone walls. You'll emerge at the sea beside the sand dunes that spread back from the shore, adjacent to *Lucky* (see p.160), and the legendary *Blue Bar* (see p.161).

Castell Romà de Can Blai

Around the 10km marker on the highway through Formentera's central strip, a signposted turn-off leads just south to the fenced-in remains of a large Roman fort, Castell Romà de Can Blai. The sandstone foundations are all that's left of the square structure, which originally had five towers. The fort guarded the island's east–west highway and the nearby port, Es Caló de Sant Agustí, but little else is known about it.

Es Caló de Sant Agustí

Bus from La Savina, May–Oct 7 daily; Nov–April 1 daily, 15min. Nestled around a rocky niche in the north coast, 2km east of the Castell Romà, the tiny cove of Es Caló de Sant Agustí has served as nearby La Mola's fishing port since Roman times. Sitting snug below the cliffs of La Mola, this diminutive harbour consists of a tiny, rocky, semicircular bay ringed by the rails of fishing huts. It's a pretty enough scene, but there's no real reason to stop other than for Es Caló's two excellent fish restaurants, *Rafalet* (see p.161) and *Pascual* (see p.160).

The shallow water surrounding Es Caló does offer decent snorkelling; head for the heavily eroded limestone rocks that ring the bay to the south. If you're after a beach, scramble 300m over the rocks (or take the signposted turn-off from the highway) to the inviting sands at **Ses Platgetes**, where you'll also find a good *kiosko* selling snacks and drinks.

La Mola

The knuckle-shaped tableland of La Mola, the island's eastern tip, is the most scenic part of Formentera, combining dense forest with traditionally farmed countryside. La Mola's limestone promontory looks down on the rest of the island from a high point of 192m, and there are stunning views across the ocean from the steep cliffs that have given La Mola's inhabitants protection on three sides since the area was first settled around 2000 BC.

From Es Caló de Sant Agustí, the highway dips before beginning the long climb up La Mola, passing a signposted left turn after 500m for Camí Romà, or "Roman Way", a beautiful but steep pathway up to La Mola, which was part of the original Roman road across Formentera. It offers hikers a refreshingly shady and traffic-free shortcut up the hill. The highway's steep incline continues past the Mar i Land turn-off, winding through Formentera's largest forest via a series of hairpin bends that will exhaust all but the fittest cyclists. At the 14km marker is the *El Mirador* restaurant (see p.160), from where there are sublime sunset views, after which the road levels out.

Mar i Land

Bus from La Savina May–Oct 7 daily; Nov–April 1 daily; 20min. Close to the highway's 13km marker, you can turn off right for the upmarket enclave of Mar i Land (also spelled "Maryland"), where two huge hotel complexes spill down a hillside towards the easternmost section of Platja de Migjorn beach (see also p.155). This section of shoreline, known as **Es Arenals**, is usually

▲ESGLÉSIA DEL PILAR DE LA MOLA

4–9pm) is held in the village's small central plaza. Much of the jewellery and craftwork is made locally, and tends to be far more imaginative than a lot of the junk on sale in Ibizan hippy markets; there's usually some live music towards the end of the day as well.

Two hundred metres east of the market plaza is the village church, **Església del Pilar de la Mola**. Built between 1772 and 1784 to a typically Ibizan design, it's the usual minimalist, whitewashed Pitiusan edifice, with a single-arched side porch and a simple belfry.

The only other sights around La Mola are two ancient **windmills** on the eastern outskirts, formerly used for grinding wheat. By the 1960s, these windmills had fallen into disuse and became hippy communes – Bob Dylan is said to have lived inside eighteenth-century **Molí Vell** for several months. Though you can't go inside the windmill today, it has been well restored and its warped wooden sails are still capable of turning the grindstone.

the most crowded spot on the southern coast. Although there are lifeguards on duty here between May and September, take care if you go for a swim, as the currents can be unpredictable.

El Pilar de la Mola

Bus from La Savina via Sant Francesc, May–Oct 4 daily; Nov–April 1 daily; extra service on market days at 5pm from La Savina via Sant Francesc, Sant Ferran, and Es Pujols, return service leaves La Mola at 7pm; 25min. The region's solitary village, and social centre for the farmers and bohemian types who make up most of the area's population, El Pilar de la Mola is a modest, pleasantly unspoiled settlement of around fifty houses, a handful of stores and a few simple bar-cafés strung along the main highway. Most of the time it's a very subdued little place, though there's a flurry of activity on Wednesdays and Sundays in the summer season, when an **art market** (May to late Sept

Far de la Mola

It's a quick straight dash through flat farmland, planted with hardy vines, to the Far de la Mola lighthouse, set in glorious seclusion at Formentera's eastern tip, Punta de la Mola. The whitewashed structure, which has a 37-kilometre beam, is something of a local landmark, and was the inspiration for the "lighthouse at the end of the world" in Jules Verne's novel *Journey Around the Solar System*. Verne was obviously taken by the wild isolation of the site, and there's a stone monument to him beside the house. There's

▲FAR DE LA MOLA

also an excellent café-bar here, *Es Puig* (see p.161).

Hotels

Hostal Bahía

Passeig de la Marina, La Savina ☎971 322 142, ⓦwww.guiaformentera. com/bahia. On the east side of La Savina's harbour this medium-sized hotel offers bright, airy and spacious rooms, all with air con and TV; some have private balconies, while others share a large terrace. There's a reasonable café-restaurant downstairs. €88–128.

Hostal La Savina

Avgda Mediterránea 22–40, La Savina ☎ & ⓕ971 322 279, ⓔhostallasavina@terra.es. May–Oct. Well-run hotel, situated opposite the Estany des Peix on the main road to Sant Francesc, with access to a narrow beach area. The cheerful comfortable rooms all have air con and attractive bathrooms, and most have lake views. Buffet breakfast is included in the ground floor

bar/restaurant (which serves very good rice dishes) and there's also Internet access. €72–88.

Hostal Residencia Illes Pitiüses

Ctra La Savina–La Mola, Sant Ferran ☎971 328 189, ⓦwww.illespitiuses.com. Modern hotel with 26 good-value, spacious rooms, all with satellite TV, air con, safe and private bathroom. It's efficiently run by a helpful German management team and the only minor drawback is its location on the main cross-island road, though traffic noise is not that noticeable. Parking available, and there's a café downstairs. €43–60.

Hostal Residencia Mar Blau

Es Caló de Sant Agustí ☎ & ⓕ971 327 030. April–Oct. Excellent small hotel, next to the fishing harbour and near Ses Platgetes beach. The bright, attractive rooms are good value and there are also high-quality apartments next door that sleep up to four (the latter costing from €91). €66–80.

Hostal Residencia Mayans

Es Pujols ☎ & ⓕ971 328 724. May–Oct. Pleasant *hostal* in a quiet spot 100m away from the main resort area. The rooms are modern and agreeably decorated and all have private bathrooms; book one on the upper floors for panoramic sea or island views. There's a pool, and the terrace café downstairs serves a popular buffet breakfast. €70.

Pensions

Hostal Centro

Plaça de sa Constitució, Sant Francesc Xavier ☎971 322 063. Budget *hostal* across the square from the church, with seven simply furnished double rooms. The large adjacent restaurant serves reasonable and inexpensive snacks and meals. €36.

Pension Bon Sol

c/Major 84–90, Sant Ferran ☎971 328 882. April–Oct. One of the cheapest places on Formentera, this place is just south of Sant Ferran's plaza. The basic but clean rooms are fairly spacious and located above a friendly bar; bathrooms are shared. €32.

Apartments

Casitas Ca Marí

Es Ca Marí, Platja de Migjorn ☎971 328 180, ☎971 328 229. May–Oct. A stone's throw from the western end of one of Formentera's best beaches, this complex has 32 simple, self-catering bungalows, sleeping up to four, all with pine furniture and small terraces. €70.

Shops

Formentera Tattoo

c/d'Espardell, Es Pujols, Formentera Moderately priced surf and skate wear, jewellery, and has an in-store tattoo parlour.

Summertime

c/Pla de Rei 59, Sant Francesc Xavier. Small fashion boutique with a good selection of colourful, stylish summer gear for women.

Cafés

Café Martinal

c/Archiduc Salvador 18, Sant Francesc Xavier. Mon–Sat 8am–3pm. In the heart of the capital, this is by far the most popular breakfast café in Formentera, with healthy set menus that include fresh juices, yoghurt and muesli, plus mini-*bocadillos*.

Fonda Platé

c/Santa Maria, Sant Francesc Xavier. Mon–Sat 10am–1am. Inviting place with a great vine-shaded terrace facing Sant Francesc's pretty central square. There's also a lofty, beamed interior with

▼ CAFÉ MARTINAL

▲RESTAURANT PASCUAL

pinball, pool and bar football. The extensive menu includes tapas, salads, pasta and good juices.

Lucky

Platja de Migjorn. May–Oct daily 10am–sunset Excellent Italian run *chiringuito*, smack in the middle of glorious Platja de Migjorn beach, with a short menu of well-prepared salads (try the fig and goats' cheese) and fresh pasta, plus fine downbeat tunes. To get here, take the turn-off at km 8 on the La Savina–La Mola road, and *Lucky* is signposted once you reach the shore.

Restaurants

Aigua

La Savina ☎971 323 322. April–Oct daily 1–4pm & 7pm–midnight. Smart harbourside bar/restaurant that's an occasional venue for chillout events, with stylish seating and a large terrace. Offers quite pricey Spanish and European cuisine, including grilled meat and fish, salads and a better-value *menú del día*. Never seems to get very busy.

El Mirador

La Savina–La Mola road, km 14 ☎971 327 037. May–Oct daily 1–4pm & 7–11pm. This moderately priced popular spot has jaw-dropping vistas over the entire western half of the island from its terrace, and an inexpensive menu – the salad with bread and dried fish is a Formenteran speciality and there's plenty of grilled meats and fish. Book ahead in July and August for a table with a sunset view.

La Pequeña Isla

El Pilar de la Mola ☎971 327 068. May–Oct 1–4pm & 8–11.30pm; Nov–April 7.30–11pm. Inexpensive, dependable roadside village bar/restaurant, known for its well-prepared Formenteran cooking – roast rabbit, sausages, squid in its own ink and plenty of rice-based dishes – served on a covered outside terrace, or in the dining area at the rear.

Restaurant Pascual

Caló de Sant Agustí ☎971 327 014. April–Oct 1–4pm & 7–11pm. Long-running, very welcoming seafood restaurant that is consistently recommended by Fomenterans. There's no sea view, but for around €25–30 per person you can feast on terrific spiny (or Norwegian) lobster or the paella-like *arròs a la banda* on a terrace underneath pine trees.

Restaurant Rafalet

Caló de Sant Agustí ☏ 971 327 077. May–Sept daily 1–4pm & 7–11.30pm. This excellent place is divided into two. The casual, inexpensive bar area's speciality is *pa amb coses* ("bread and things") which may include cheese, pork loin, tortilla, olives and green peppers, for around €12 per person. *Rafalet*'s other half is one of the finest fish restaurants in the Pitiuses, set right on the water's edge, with a comprehensive, fairly pricey menu that includes paella and *bollit de peix* (rice dish with red mullet), and perfectly grilled squid, sole or prawns.

Rigatoni

Es Pujols ☏ 971 328 351. May–Oct daily 1–4pm & 8pm–midnight. Midway along Es Pujol's beach, with a huge shoreside terrace, this stylish, enjoyable Italian-owned restaurant serves fine fresh pasta and great fish dishes, plus good salads and great *gelati*.

Bars

Bar Verdera

Sant Ferran. Daily 6.30am–1.30am. Also known as *Los Currantes*, this unreconstructed, scruffy locals' bar initially looks pretty unappealing but it does have an excellent and very inexpensive selection of tapas. It's right on the main highway with roadside seating.

Blue Bar

Platja de Migjorn ☏ 971 187 011, ⊛ www.bluebarformentera.com. April–Oct daily noon–4am. Sublime

chillout bar with a terrific location amongst the sand dunes above Platja Migjorn. Once a hippy stronghold, the *Blue Bar* is now something of an ambient HQ, with inspirational electronic sounds pumped out over the wooden-decked terrace. The menu includes salads and pasta; book a table in advance, but be prepared to wait for your food. The signposted turn-off for the bar is at km 8 on the La Savina–La Mola road.

▲BLUE BAR

Es Puig

Punta de la Mola. Daily May–Oct 9am–10pm; Nov–April 9am–6pm. The bar at the end of the world, right next to the Far de la Mola lighthouse, and famous for its *platos de jamón y queso* – huge portions of local and Menorcan cheese, cured ham and salami. It's also *the* place to wait for the first sunrise of the New Year, when the bar stays open all night.

Fonda Pepe

c/Major, Sant Ferran. May–Oct & Christmas–New Year daily 8am–3am. Steeped in hippy folklore, this legendary drinking den was once *the* happening bar in Formentera; nostalgia reigns in the bar, with photos and doodles from the 1960s on the walls. It's enjoyable enough and busy in summer, when the

Formentera PLACES

▼FONDA PEPE

narrow terrace is packed with (mainly German) visitors. The adjoining *Peyka* restaurant is open for dinner only.

Riamblu

Es Pujols–Sant Ferran road. May–Oct 7pm–4am. Stylish bar on the outskirts of Es Pujols that's the best bet for a pre-clubbing wind up, with a huge terrace, modish lighting, and soul, funk and melodic house sounds from island-based and visiting DJs.

Clubs

Xueño

Es Pujols–Sant Ferran road. June–Sept. Formentera's only club – renamed *Xueño* and revitalized by a new Italian management team – is an intimate (capacity 400), stylish venue with a main room, terrace and chillout zone. Premier league house music talent now visits the island to perform at the club – DJs Sharam from Deep Dish, Bob Sinclar, and singers Barbara Tucker and Robert Owens have all performed here, alongside regular DJs Buti, Pippi and Claudio Coccoluto. Draws a mixed Italian/local crowd; entrance and bar prices are moderate.

Amnesia trip

In high season, a special boat is chartered by Italian promoters *Made in Italy* to ferry people from Formentera to Ibiza for their weekly residency nights at *Amnesia*, leaving around 10pm and returning at 6am; the latest schedule is available at the ferry terminal in La Savina.

Essentials

Arrival

Ibiza Airport (☎ 971 809 000) is 7km south of Ibiza Town and well served by buses (#10; hourly 7.30am–10.30pm; €1) all year round. Taxis charge approximately €11 to Ibiza Town, €18 to Sant Antoni or €20 to Santa Eulària; prices rise a little after 9pm. Virtually all package holidays include a free transfer to your hotel. There's no airport in **Formentera**, but regular ferries and hydrofoils shuttle between the two islands, mostly from Ibiza Town (see p.148).

International **ferries** from mainland Spain dock at Passeig Marítim on the south side of Ibiza Town's harbour. At the time of writing there was also a direct weekly ferry to La Savina, Formentera.

Note that travel connections to both islands are much poorer in **winter**. At the time of research there was only one airline (Air Berlin) flying between Ibiza and the UK between November and April, though other carriers offer alternative routes via Palm and Barcelona.

Information and maps

The best information about Ibiza and Formentera is available from tourist information offices on the islands, and from the Internet. In Ibiza, there are **tourist offices** at the airport (May–Sept Mon–Sat 9am–2pm & 4–9pm; Sun 9am–2pm; ☎ 971 809 118), in Ibiza Town (see p.51), in Sant Antoni (see p.109) and Santa Eulària (see p.81), in addition to the small kiosks (all May–Oct only) located in many resorts. There's also a helpful office in La Savina, Formentera (see p.148). All staff speak English, and can provide leaflets and accommodation lists.

On the **web**, try the excellent Ibiza Spotlight (🖰 www.ibiza-spotlight. com) or 🖰 www.guiaformentera.com for Formentera. The Balearic Islands' website (🖰 www.visitbalears.com) is worth a look, with features, news and events in separate sections devoted to Ibiza and Formentera. The Spanish Tourist Board (🖰 www.tourspain.es) only has very general background detail about the Pitiuses.

All the main British **newspapers** are widely available. For local news, the DIY journalism peddled by the *Ibiza Sun*, a free newssheet available in all resorts and at 🖰 www.theibizasun.net is pretty rough-and-ready but does cover the main stories in reasonable depth; the pedestrian monthly *Ibiza Now* is geared towards the ageing ex-pat market. There are two free monthly English language magazines, dedicated mostly to Ibiza club culture and style, of which the glossy, informative *Pacha* is the best by a long way; *DJ Magazine* (an offshoot of the UK publication) is the also ran and very San An-oriented.

The best **map** of Ibiza is published by Kompass (1:50,000). Of those available in Ibiza, Joan Costa (1:70,000) is the one to go for. Most car rental companies will provide you with a reasonable free map. Serious hikers should pick up copies of the IGN 1:25,000 maps, available at Transit, c/d'Aragó 45, Ibiza Town.

Transport

Ibiza has a pretty good transport network, with regular public **buses** and **boats** linking all the main resorts and towns, and there's a decent bus service on Formentera considering its tiny population. If you're planning on really exploring the islands, however, you're going to have to rent a **car**, **motorbike** or a **bicycle**, as many of the best stretches of coastline are well off the beaten track.

Buses

Buses in Ibiza and Formentera are inexpensive, punctual and will get you around fairly quickly. Services between the main towns and resorts run roughly from 7.30am to midnight between June and late September, and 7.30am until 9.30pm in winter. Smaller villages and resorts are less well served, and buses to them are very infrequent in winter. Services to the more popular beaches and resorts are increased between June and late September. **Timetables** are available in tourist offices, printed in local newspapers and available at ® www .ibizabus.com. Note that there are many fewer buses on Sundays on all routes.

From **Ibiza Town**, there are buses to all the main towns, most villages and many resorts, and to Salines beach all year round. **Sant Antoni** and **Santa Eulària** are the other two transport hubs, with frequent services to local beach resorts and good intra-island connections. In **Formentera** buses shuttle between Es Pujols, Sant Ferran, Sant Francesc and La Savina, and there's also a route across the island, from La Savina to La Mola. **Fares** are very reasonable on all routes: Ibiza Town–Sant Antoni costs €1.50, while the longest route, Ibiza Town–Portinatx, is €2.30.

Between mid-June and late September the all-night **discobus** service provides hourly shuttles between Ibiza Town and Sant Antoni (passing *Amnesia* and *Privilege*); Ibiza Town and Platja d'en

Bossa (for *Space*); Sant Antoni and Port des Torrent; Es Canar and Santa Eulària; and Santa Eulària and Ibiza Town. During the rest of the year, the same buses run on Saturday nights only. Tickets cost €1.50; for more information, call ®971 192 456.

Tourist train

The "**tourist train**", a mock steam locomotive with carriages that whisk you up into the hills around Santa Agnès, leaves from the harbourfront promenade in Sant Antoni (June–Sept daily at 11am, 1pm and 4pm; no Sun services in July and Aug; 1hr 50min return trip; adults €10, under-12s €5).

Boats

Plenty of **boats** buzz up and down the Ibizan coastline between May and late September, providing a delightful – if more expensive – alternative to bus travel. Services go from Ibiza Town to Talamanca and Platja d'en Bossa; from Sant Antoni to Sant Antoni bay, Cala Bassa and Cala Conta; and from Santa Eulària to northeast beaches, including Es Canar. Fares range from roughly €3– 7. For ferry and hydrofoil connections between Ibiza Town and Formentera see p.148.

Taxis

Taxi rates on both islands are quite pricey, though all have meters and tariffs are fixed. There's a minimum charge of €2.85, with additional charges after 9pm, on Sundays and public holidays, and to or from the airport or docks. Ibiza Town to Sant Antoni (15km) will cost about €17, while to get to Sant Rafel (for *Amnesia* or *Privilege*) from either Ibiza Town or Sant Antoni at night is around

€11. The latest fares are posted on ⓦwww.taxi-eivissa.com.

Taxis for hire display a green light – you can hail them on the street, wait at one of the designated ranks, or call (see numbers below). You'll have no problems getting a taxi at most times of the year, but demand far exceeds supply on most August nights, when it's not uncommon to wait up to an hour for a ride. It's well worth bearing in mind that all Ibiza clubs will pay your taxi fare from anywhere on the island if four of the passengers purchase an entrance ticket to the venue.

Taxi companies

Ibiza Town ☎971 398 483, ☎971 301 794, ☎971 306 602.
La Savina, Formentera ☎971 322 002.
Sant Antoni ☎971 340 074, ☎971 343 764.
Santa Eulària ☎971 330 063.
Sant Francesc, Formentera ☎971 322 016.
Sant Joan ☎971 800 243.
Es Pujols, Formentera ☎971 328 016.

Car and motorbike rental

Driving along Ibiza and Formentera's main roads is pretty straightforward, though to really see the islands you'll have to tackle some challenging dirt tracks from time to time. Take particular care on the notorious Sant Antoni–Ibiza Town highway at night, where fatal accidents are all too common.

Daily **car rental** costs are reasonable: for the cheapest small hatchback, expect to pay around €33 a day in July and August, and around €27 per day the rest of the year. Local companies are usually less expensive than the international brands. Note that it's essential to book a car in advance in August due to high demand. You have to be over 21 years old to rent a car in Spain.

Motorbikes and **scooters** are also a popular means of getting around the islands independently, with rates starting at around €30 for the cheapest motorbike, or from €18 a day for a scooter model. In low-lying Formentera, even the least powerful model will be adequate to get two people around, but to explore hilly Ibiza you should hire a machine above 100cc. Legally, you must be over eighteen to rent a motorbike over 75cc, and crash helmets are compulsory.

Vehicle **insurance policies** vary but it's essential to ensure you have full cover (all the companies listed below include this in their contracts). Check the excess waiver amount – obviously, the higher the rate specified in the contract, the more you'll have to pay if you're involved in an accident. Note that most insurance policies cover you for neither breakdowns nor accidents on dirt roads.

Local car and motorbike rental companies

Autos Marí c/de la Mar 25, Santa Eulària ☎971 330 236, ☎971 332 659; **Canals Albert** Avgda Dr. Fleming, Sant Antoni ☎971 345 571.
Moto Luis Avgda Portmany 5, Sant Antoni ☎971 340 521, ⓦwww.motoluis.com.
Isla Blanca c/Felipe II, Ibiza Town ☎971 315 407; La Savina, Formentera ☎971 322 559.

International car rental companies

Avis ☎971 396 453, ⓦwww.avis.com.
Budget ☎971 395 982, ⓦwww.budget.com.
Hertz ☎971 396 018, ⓦwww.hertz.com.
National ☎971 395 393, ⓦwww.nationalcar.com.

Cycling

With few hills, **Formentera** is perfect bicycle territory and **cycling** is an easy and popular way to get around the island. Pick up a *Green Routes* leaflet from the tourist office for details of some good, well-signposted cycle excursions along the island's quieter lanes. **Ibiza** is much more hilly, and its roads more congested, though there are some spectacular dirt track routes across the island, perfect for mountain biking. A network of signposted routes is currently being developed; contact tourist information offices for leaflets. In both islands, renting bikes starts at around €8 a day, while state-of-the-art mountain bikes cost about €11 and kids' bikes around €6.

Kandani (see below) and Ecoibiza, c/Abad i Lasierra 35, Ibiza Town (℡ 971 302 347; ⓦ www.ecoibiza. com), organize **mountain-bike tours**. Ecoibiza's half-day tours start at €38 and a tour of Formentera costs €54. If you're interested in serious mountain-

bike racing, consult the website ⓦ www. ibizabtt.com for details of events.

Bike rental

Autos Ca Mari La Savina, Formentera ℡ 971 322 921.
Bicicletas/Moto Rent Mitjorn La Savina, Formentera ℡ 971 322 306.
Kandani Ctra Es Canar 109, Santa Eulària ℡ & ℻ 971 339 264 ⓦ www.ibiza-activa. com.
Tony Rent c/Navarra 11, Ibiza Town ℡ 971 300 879.

Sports and leisure

You'll find plenty of opportunity for **sports and leisure activities** in Ibiza and Formentera, from yoga to horse riding. With a sparkling coastline never more than a short drive away, watersports are especially good. Coastal Ibiza and Formentera also offer superb scenery for hikers.

Swimming and beach life

Swimming in Ibiza and Formentera is absolutely wonderful with dozens of Blue Flag beaches and unpolluted, clear and – for much of the year – warm water to enjoy. Sea temperatures are at their lowest in February (around 15°C), and highest in early September (around 25°C).

All resort beaches, and most family-oriented bays have umbrellas (€3–5 per day) and sunbeds (€3 per day) for rent. You'll also find pedolos (around €8 per hour), and many beaches, including Cala Bassa (see p.118) and Platja d'en Bossa (see p.137), offer banana boat rides (around €9 per trip).

Diving and snorkelling

The Pitiusan islands boast some of the cleanest seas in the Mediterranean, their coastlines dotted with blue-flag beaches. With little rainfall runoff, the water is exceptionally clear for most of the year and visibility of up to 40m is quite common.

Scuba diving is generally excellent, with warm seas and (mostly) gentle currents. Boats tend to head for the tiny offshore islands such as Tagomago and Espardell that ring the coasts, where sea life is at its most diverse. Schools of barracuda and large groupers are often seen, and you can expect to spot conger and moray eels, plenty of colourful wrasse, plus crabs and octopuses. There are also three shipwrecks around Illot Llado near Ibiza Town and another in Cala Mastella, plus caves and crevices all around the coastline to investigate. Most scuba-diving schools open between May and September only (those that open longer are noted below) and tend to charge similar prices. A single boat-dive works out at around €40–45 including all equipment, or there are discounts for packages of six or ten dives. If you want to **learn to dive**, expect to pay €360–

430 for a five-day PADI Open Water course. You'll find a BSAC school in Port des Torrent, and there's a decompression chamber in Ibiza Town.

Small coves and rocky shorelines offer the most productive **snorkelling** territory: try Cala Mastella, Cala Molí and Cala Codolar in Ibiza, or Caló de Sant Agustí in Formentera. Perhaps the best area for experienced snorkellers and freedivers is the rugged northwest Ibizan coastline, at bays such as Es Portitxol and Cala d'Aubarca, where there are very steep drop-offs and deep, clear water. You'll often encounter coastal fish such as ballan, goby, grouper, brown and painted wrasse, as well as passing pelagic sea life such as mackerel or even barracuda. Most resorts have a store where you can buy snorkelling **equipment**, but as much of it is poor quality, it's well worth renting or buying from a dive school or a specialist fishing store.

Scuba diving centres

Diving Centre San Miguel *Hotel Cartago,* Port de Sant Miquel ☎971 334 539, ⌨www.divingcenter-sanmiguel.com. Scuba school with inexpensive rates (€345 for a dive licence), though not PADI affiliated.
Formentera Diving and Watersports La Savina, Formentera ☎971 323 232. One of Formentera's best dive schools; also rents out kayaks, jet skis and boats.
Ibiza Diving Port Esportiu, Santa Eulària ☎971 332 949, ⌨www.ibiza-diving.com. Five-star PADI school, with Nitrox training course and underwater scooters available.
Sea Horse Sub Port des Torrent ☎971 346 438 ⌨www.seahorsedivingibiza. com. BSAC-accredited dive school offering dives inside the Cala d'Hort Natural Park. May–Oct.
Sirena c/Balanzat 21, Sant Antoni ☎971 342 966, ⌨www.ibiza-online.com/Diving-Sirena. Training courses and trips to Ibiza's west coast sites.
Subfari Es Portitxol beach, Cala Portinatx ☎971 333 183. Scuba school that offers dives at many of Ibiza's remote north coast sites.
Vellmari Marina Botafoc 101–2, Ibiza Town ☎971 192 884; Avgda Mediterráneo 90, La Savina, Formentera ☎971 322 105; ⌨www.vellmari.com. Five-star PADI

dive centres that run daily trips into the Ses Salines natural park; the Ibiza branch is open all year.

Windsurfing and sailing

Windsurfing and **sailing** are popular in the Pitiuses – July and August are often the calmest months, so less challenging for the experienced, but conditions are excellent for much of the year. In early and late summer, the southern sirocco wind reaches Force 4 about once a week, while the westerly mistral can blow in at Force 6. The most popular beaches include Cala Martina (ideal for beginners) just north of Santa Eulària, Platja d'en Bossa and Cala Conta (for the more advanced surfer). Windsurf board rental costs around €16 per hour and training courses around €23 per hour.

Windsurfing and sailing centres

Club de Surf Ibiza Platja d'en Bossa ☎971 192 418. Long-established wind-surfing school, offering board rental and tuition.
Club Delfin Vela y Windsurf *Hotel Delfin,* Cala Codolar ☎971 806 210. Sailing school offering windsurf tuition and board rental.
Vela Náutica Avgda Dr. Fleming, Sant Antoni ☎971 346 535. Windsurfing equipment, sailing boats and kayaks for rent.

Boat trips and deep-sea fishing

Pleasure-boat trips around the coastline are highly popular, and available in most Ibizan resorts. The Ibiza to Formentera day-trip is the most popular of these, costing €19–26 and usually leaving around 9.30am and returning by 6pm. Most stop at Espalmador island before continuing to Platja Illetes, and often La Savina.

Other excursions leaving from the Sant Antoni harbour (all bookable from the harbourfront) include a three-hour return trip to Es Vedrà (daily €15) passing

Atlantis and including a snorkelling stop in Cala d'Hort, and a day-trip up the northwest coastline to Portinatx, passing many isolated coves; boats sail twice weekly, €20 return). In Formentera, Cruceros, La Savina (☎ 971 323 207) organize excellent half-day (€50 per person) and full-day (€75) trips on a catamaran around the island; prices include a gourmet lunch.

It's not that expensive to **charter** a boat. The English owners of *La Vida de Riley* catamaran (☎ 629 007 356, ⊛ www. sail-ibiza.com) offer an excellent range of flexible trips including day-trips to Formentera and sunset cruises, with pick-ups from any Ibiza beach; prices start at €25 per person. Tagomago Charters, Port Esportiu, Santa Eulària (☎ 971 338 101) have several boats, from simple tub-like craft with an outboard motor (€210 per day) to swanky Sunseekers (€4000 a day); add on €150 for a skipper.

Deep sea fishing is another popular sport; Pesca Ibiza, Edificio Bristol, Avgda 8 d'Agost, Ibiza Town (☎ 971 314 491), organizes trawling and bottom fishing excursions from €110 per person for a half-day trip.

Hiking

Ibiza and Formentera's beautiful coastal paths and inland valleys offer exceptional **hiking**. We've detailed a few of the best walks within the Guide, which all have opportunities for a swim along the way; trainers and shorts are adequate equipment. If you plan on doing a lot of walking, IGN (see p.165) publish the most useful maps, and the locally published *Ibiza Now* hiking guides are pretty decent, though only available in Ibiza (from most bookshops and newsagents).

The quality of the Ibizan tourist offices' hiking leaflets is improving but is still not that reliable, and the signpost network that should accompany them is incomplete at the time of research. Things are better organized in Formentera where the Green Routes network has good waymarked tracks suitable for hikers and

bikers (leaflets available from the tourist office in La Savina).

Ecoibiza, c/Abad y Lasierra 35, Ibiza Town (☎ 971 302 347, ⊛ www.ecoibiza. com) arranges some good "Secret Walks" to remote parts of the island, including some superb hikes around Santa Agnès; half-day trips cost €28 per person; full-day excursions are €34–45.

Horse riding

In Ibiza, Easy Riders (☎ 971 196 511), located 200m along the Sòl d'en Serra from Cala Llonga, has some fine horses and offers thrilling countryside and beach and hill rides; a fifty-minute trek costs €20 while an hour and forty minutes is €38. You could also try Can Mayans, Santa Gertrudis–Sant Llorenç road, km 3 (☎ 971 187 388), who charge €15 per hour for countryside rides.

Go-karting

There are two **go-kart tracks** in Ibiza; the hilly 300m Santa Eulària circuit, Ibiza Town–Santa Eulària road, km 5.8 (daily March–Oct 10am–sunset; ☎ 971 317 744), is the better option, with speedy 400cc adult karts (€20 for 7min), junior karts (€7 for 7min) and baby karts (€3 for 5min). Much flatter and less scenic, the second track is just outside Sant Antoni along the highway to Ibiza Town (daily May–Oct noon–midnight) and has similar prices.

Golf

The only **golf** course in the Pitiuses is Club de Golf Ibiza (☎ 971 196 152), halfway along the Jesús–Santa Eulària highway at Roca Llisa. It boasts a nine- and an eighteen-hole course, both positioned between patches of pine woodlands under the island's central hills. You don't have to be a member to play, but it's an expensive course – green fees are €78, and you'll pay extra for a caddy and for renting a golf buggy, though the price does includes club rental.

Yoga

Ibiza is fast establishing itself as one of the Mediterranean's key **yoga** destinations, with a choice of centres run by acclaimed instructors. The island itself, with its benign climate and stunning scenery, makes an inspirational base, with many classes performed in the open air in rural surrounds. All prices quoted below exclude flights and transfers.

Yoga centres

Ibiza Yoga Benirràs, Ibiza; UK ☎020 7419 0999, ⊛www.ibizayoga.com; open all year. Highly popular Ashtanga yoga

retreat, situated in a spectacular location a short walk south from one of Ibiza's finest beaches, with seafood restaurants close by for evening meals. Weekly rates are £375–750 per person (depending on the villa and season) for villa accommodation and three hours of tuition per day, breakfast and lunch. Pagodas (£395 per person) teepees (£225–375) and a gazebo (£350–425) are also available on the same deal; day yoga passes cost £25 and a week yoga-only pass £135.

Jivana Ashram 1km inland from Cala Conta (☎971 342 494; May–Oct). Small Ashtanga yoga retreat run by friendly, experienced German instructors; there's a maximum of eight per class. Accommodation is in comfortable double rooms, but there's no electricity, so it's an early-to-bed kind of place. Superb beaches are only a short walk away. The weekly rate, including full board, is €360; a half-day class costs €20.

Festivals and events

While Ibiza and Formentera cannot claim to host particularly extravagant **festivals**, what celebrations there are form an important part of the social calendar and present the chance for family get-togethers. Every settlement holds an annual *festa* to celebrate the patron saint of the community, with religious services and cultural events in the village square. All of the *festas* listed below follow a similar pattern, with Ibizan *ball pagès* (folk dancing) and often a display from another region of Spain, plus some live music of the soft rock variety. Bonfires are lit, *torradas* (barbecues) spit and sizzle, traditional sweet snacks like *bunyols* and *orelletes* are prepared, and there's always plenty of alcohol to lubricate proceedings. Some of the bigger events, like Sant Bartomeu celebrations in Sant Antoni on August 24th and the *Anar a Maig* in Santa Eulària involve spectacular fireworks displays.

"*Molts anys i bons*" (many years and good ones) is the customary festival toast.

January
Festa de Sant Antoni Jan 17, Ibiza.
Festa de Santa Agnès de Corona Jan 21, Ibiza.

February/March
Festa de Santa Eulària Feb 12, Ibiza.
Carnaval Towns and villages on both islands live it up during the week before Lent with marches, fancy-dress parades and classical music concerts.

March/April
Semana Santa Holy Week is widely observed, with thousands assembling to watch the religious processions through Dalt Vila, Ibiza Town and up to the Puig de Missa in Santa Eulària on Good Friday.
Festa de Sant Francesc March 2, Ibiza.
Festa de Sant Josep March 19, Ibiza.
Festa de Sant Vicent April 5, Ibiza.
Festa de Sant Jordi April 23, Ibiza. Traditional fiesta in Sant Jordi, Ibiza and book-giving throughout the Pitiuses to mark the day.

Water worship

In addition to the religious festivals, water-worshipping ceremonies (*xacotes pageses*) are performed at springs (*fonts*) and wells (*pous*) throughout the Pitiusan countryside, but particularly in Ibiza. These festivals are thought to be Carthaginian in origin, and involve much singing and dancing, in order to give thanks for water in islands plagued by droughts. Some better-known ceremonies include:

July 25 Pou d'en Benet, Benimussa, 4km east of Sant Antoni.
Aug 5 Font des Verger, Es Cubells.
First Sun after Aug 5 Pou Roig, near Sant Jordi.
First Sun after Aug 28 Pou des Rafals, Sant Agustí.
Oct 10 Pou de Forada, 5km northeast of Sant Antoni.

May

Anar a Maig First Sun in May. Large festival in Santa Eulària with processions of horse-drawn carts, classical music, a flower festival and a big fireworks finale.
Festa de Sant Ferran May 30, Formentera.

June

Nit de Sant Joan June 23. Midsummer night features huge bonfires and effigy-burning in Sant Joan, Ibiza and throughout the Pitiuses.

July

Día de Verge del Carmen July 15–16. The patron saint of seafarers and fisher-men is honoured with parades and the blessing of boats, especially in La Savina, Formentera and Ibiza Town, where the Verge del Carmen statue is removed from the Església Sant Elm by the fishermen of La Marina and placed in a boat, which then leads a flotilla around the harbour in a ceremony to ask her protection at sea for the year ahead.
Festa de Sant Jaume July 25. Widely celebrated throughout Formentera.

August

Santa Maria de las Neus Aug 5. Cel-ebrated with a special mass in Ibiza Town's cathedral.
Festa de Sant Ciriac Aug 8. Small ceremony in Dalt Vila, Ibiza Town to commemorate the reconquest of 1235, plus a massive watermelon fight in Es Soto below the walls.

Día de Sant Bartomeu Aug 24. Huge harbourside fireworks display, plus concerts and dancing, in Sant Antoni, Ibiza.
Festa de Sant Agustí Aug 28, Ibiza.

September

Festa de Jesús Sept 8, Ibiza.
Festa de Sant Mateu Sept 21, Ibiza.

October

Verge del Pilar Oct 12, La Mola, Formentera.
Festa de Santa Teresa Oct 15, Es Cubells, Ibiza.
Festa de Sa Creu Oct 24, Sant Rafel, Ibiza. Locally made ceramics are displayed and for sale.

November

Festa de Sant Carles Nov 4, Ibiza.
Festa de Santa Gertrudis Nov 16, Ibiza. Includes prize animal exhibits.

December

Wine festival First weekend in Dec, Sant Mateu, Ibiza. A tremendously sociable event, with crowds sampling the vintage from teapot-shaped glass jugs called *porros*, and feasting on barbecued *sobrassada* and *butifarra* sausages.
Día de Sant Francesc Dec 5, Formentera.
Christmas (*Nadal*) Candlelight services throughout the Pitiuses.
New Year (*Cap d'Any*) Big parties in night-clubs and Vara de Rey, Ibiza, traditionally celebrated in Spain by eating twelve grapes, one on each strike of the clock at midnight.

Directory

Accommodation Unless otherwise stated all accommodation listed throughout the Places chapters is open all year. The price range indicates the cost of the cheapest double room in high season (June–Sept), including taxes; this price can vary substantially as costs are generally much higher in August.

Addresses Most street names are in Catalan, though some Castilian names survive: Plaça des Parc is Plaza del Parque on some maps. Common abbreviations are c/ for Carrer or Calle (street), Ctra for Carretera (highway). Note that in Spain, businesses located on main roads use kilometre markers to indicate their location; so the restaurant *Can Caus* adopts the address Ibiza Town–Santa Gertrudis, km 3.5. This means that the restaurant is located 3.5km from the beginning of the road between Ibiza Town and Santa Gertrudis.

Airlines Air Berlin ☏901 116 402, ⊛www.airberlin.com; Air Europa ☏902 401 501, ⊛www.air-europa.com; BMIbaby ☏971 395 565, ⊛www.bmibaby.com; easyJet ☏902 29 99 92, ⊛www.easyjet. com; First Choice Airways ☏971 394 621, ⊛www.firstchoice.co.uk/flights; GB Airways ☏902 111 333, ⊛www.gbairways.com; Iberia ☏902 400 500, ⊛www.iberia.com; Spanair ☏902 929 191, ⊛www.spanair. es; Vueling ☏902 333 933, ⊛www. vueling.com.

Banks and exchange Spain's currency is the euro (€). Cashpoints (ATMs) are extremely widespread and accept all the main credit and debit cards. Banks offer the best rates for changing travellers' cheques and foreign currency, though they have very limited banking hours (generally Mon–Sat 9am–2pm). Bureaux de change are found in all the main resorts, often staying open until midnight, but their commission rates are higher. Virtually all restaurants and large stores accept credit cards, but you'll often need your passport as ID.

Clubs Clubbing in Ibiza is inordinately expensive: entrance prices average €35–40 and can cost anything up to €60. It pays to seek out advance tickets, available in the hip bars of San An and Ibiza Town, which typically save you €6–10 (and include a free drink), or blag a guest pass if you can. Drinks are outrageously priced – soft drinks,

including bottled water cost €6–8; a spirit with a mixer anything up €15.

Consulates UK, Avgda d'Isidor Macabich 45, Ibiza Town ☏971 301 818 (Mon–Fri 9am–3pm). The nearest Irish (☏971 719 244) and US consulates (☏971 725 051) are in Mallorca.

Emergency services For the police, fire brigade or an ambulance call ☏112.

Hospital Can Misses, c/de Corona (☏971 397 000), located in the western suburbs of Ibiza Town. There's no hospital on Formentera, but the health centre (*centre de salut*), La Savina–Sant Francesc road, km 3.1 (☏971 322 357), can deal with most medical problems.

Internet All the main towns and resorts have at least one cybercafé; half an hour costs around €2.

Post Allow a week to ten days for mail within the EU, two weeks for the rest of the world. Post offices (*correu*) open between 8.30am and 1.30pm and are found in all the main towns; some souvenir shops also sell stamps.

Telephones You'll find telephone booths in all towns, villages and resorts taking cash or phonecards (which you can buy at tobacconists, newsagents and some petrol stations). Local calls in the ☏971 Balearic area are very cheap, but mobile numbers cost around €0.70 a minute. International calls can be made from booths (around €2 for five minutes) but the most cost-effective way to dial home is by using an international phonecard (available in the same outlets).

UK mobile phones work in the Balearics, though non-triband US-bought handsets may not. If you are planning a long stay, consider buying a Spanish mobile phone or use your UK mobile in Spain by buying a new SIM chip from a telecom store; *Movistar* chips cost around €50, but include €40 of calling credit.

To call Ibiza or Formentera from abroad, dial 00 plus the relevant country code (00 34 in the UK, Ireland and New Zealand; 011 34 in North America; 0011 64 in Australia), followed by the nine-digit number. To call abroad from Ibiza or Formentera, dial 00 followed by the country code (44 for the UK; 353 for Ireland; 1 for the US and Canada; 61 for Australia; 64 for New Zealand) then the area code minus its zero, and then the number.

Time Ibiza and Formentera follow CET (Central European Time) which is one hour ahead of the UK and six hours ahead of US Eastern Standard Time. Spain adopts daylight saving in winter: clocks go back in the last week in October and forward in the last week of March.

Travel agents For flights back to the UK contact specialists The Foreign Office ☎971 308 620 ⊛www.foreign-office. com or Ibiza Travel Shop ☎971 803 175 ⊛www.ibizatravelshop.com.

Language

Spanish

Because virtually everyone can speak it, Spanish has become Ibiza and Formentera's lingua franca. Until the early 1960s, when there was a mass influx of Castilian Spanish speakers, Eivissenc, the local dialect of Catalan, was the main language in the islands. Eivissenc Catalan was still spoken after the Civil War, despite the efforts of Franco, who banned the language in the media and schools across Catalan-speaking areas of eastern Spain.

However, although Catalan is still the dominant tongue in rural areas and small villages, **Castilian Spanish** is more common in the towns. Only 38 percent of Ibizan residents (a few more in Formentera) now speak Catalan, a situation the Balearic government is trying to reverse by pushing through a programme of Catalanization. Most street signs are now in Catalan, and it's the main medium of education in schools and colleges.

English-speaking visitors to Ibiza are usually able to get by without any Spanish or Catalan, as **English** is widely understood, especially in the resorts. In Formentera, the situation is slightly different: many people can speak a little English, but as most of their visitors are German and Italian, the islanders tend to learn those languages, and you may have some communication difficulties from time to time. If you want to make an effort, it's probably best to stick to learning Spanish – and maybe try to pick up a few phrases of Catalan. You'll get a good reception if you at least try to communicate in one of these languages.

For more than a brief introduction to Spanish, pick up a copy of the Rough Guide **Spanish Dictionary Phrasebook**.

Pronunciation

The rules of **pronunciation** are pretty straightforward and strictly observed. In Ibiza and Formentera, the lisp-like qualities of mainland Castilian are not at all common – *cerveza* is usually pronounced "servesa", not "thervetha". Unless there's an accent, words ending in **d**, **l**, **r** and **z** are **stressed** on the last syllable; all others on the second last. All **vowels** are pure and short; combinations have predictable results.

c is soft before **e** and **i**, hard otherwise.

g works the same way – a guttural **h** sound (like the **ch** in loch) before **e** or **i**, and a hard **g** elsewhere – *gigante* becomes "higante".

h is always silent.

j the same sound as a guttural **g**: *jamón* is pronounced "hamon".

ll sounds like an English **y**: *tortilla* is pronounced "torteeya".

n as in English unless it has a tilde (accent) over it, when it becomes **ny**: *mañana* sounds like "man-yarna".

A few Catalan phrases

When pronouncing place names, watch out especially for words with the letter **j** – it's not "Hondal" but "Jondal", as in English. Note also that **x** is almost always a "sh" sound – Xarraca is pronounced "sharrarca". The word for a hill, *puig*, is a tricky one, pronounced "pootch".

If you want to learn more, try *Parla Català* (Pia), a good English–Catalan phrase-book, together with either the Collins or Routledge dictionary. For more serious students, the excellent *Catalan in Three Months* (Stuart Poole, UK), a combined paperback and tape package, is recommended.

Greetings and responses

Hello	Hola	Not at all/You're welcome	De res
Goodbye	Adéu	Do you speak English	Parla Anglés?
Good morning	Bon dia		
Good afternoon/night	Bona tarda/nit	I (don't) speak Catalan	(No) Parlo Català
Yes	Sí	My name is...	Em dic...
No	No	What's your name?	Com es diu?
OK	Val	I am English	Sóc anglès(a)
Please	Per favor		
Thank you	Gràcies	Scottis'h	escocès(a)
See you later	Fins després	Australian	australià/ana
Sorry	Ho sento	Canadian	canadenc(a)
Excuse me	Perdoni	American	americà/ana
How are you?	Com va?	Irish	irlandès(a)
I (don't) understand	(No) ho entec	Welsh	gallès(a)

v sounds a little more like **b**, *vino* becoming "beano".

x has an **s** sound before consonants, and a normal **x** sound before vowels.

z is the same as **s**.

Basic words and phrases

Basics

Yes, No, OK	Sí, No, Vale
Please, Thank you	Por favor, Gracias
Where?, When?	¿Dónde?, ¿Cuando?
What?, How much?	¿Qué?, ¿Cuánto?
Here	Aquí
There	Allí, Allá
This, That	Esto, Eso
Now	Ahora
Then	Más tarde
Open, Closed	Abierto/a, Cerrado/a
With, Without	Con, Sin
Good, Bad	Bueno/a, Malo/a

Big, Small	Gran(de), Pequeño/a
Cheap, Expensive	Barato/a, Caro/a
Hot, Cold	Caliente, Frío/a
More, Less	Más, Menos
Today, Tomorrow	Hoy, Mañana
Yesterday	Ayer
The bill	La cuenta

Greetings and responses

Hello, Goodbye	Hola, Adiós
Good morning	Buenos días
Good afternoon/night	Buenas tardes/noches
See you later	Hasta luego
Sorry	Lo siento/disculpéme

Excuse me	Con permiso/ perdón
How are you?	¿Cómo está (usted)?
I (don't) understand	(No) entiendo
Not at all/You're welcome	De nada
Do you speak English?	¿Habla (usted) inglés?
I (don't) speak Spanish	(No) Hablo Español
My name is…	Me llamo…
What's your name?	¿Como se llama usted?
I am English	Soy inglés(a)
Scottish	escocés(a)
Australian	australiano/a
Canadian	canadiense/a
American	americano/a
Irish	irlandés(a)
Welsh	galés(a)

Hotels and transport

I want	Quiero
I'd like	Quisiera
Do you know…?	¿Sabe…?
I don't know	No sé
There is (is there?)	(¿)Hay(?)
Give me…	Deme…
Do you have…?	¿Tiene…?
…the time	…la hora
…a room	…una habitación
…with two beds/ double bed	…con dos camas/ cama matrimonial
…with shower/bath	…con ducha/baño
for one person	para una persona
for two people	para dos personas
for one night (one week)	para una noche (una semana)
It's fine	Está bien
It's too expensive	Es demasiado caro
Can one…?	¿Se puede…?
camp (near) here?	¿…acam-par aqui (cerca)?
It's not very far	No es muy lejos
How do I get to…?	¿Por donde se va a…?
Left	Izquierda
Right	Derecha
Straight on	Todo recto
Where is.?	¿Dónde está…?
…the bus station	…la estación de autobuses
…the bus stop	…la parada
…the nearest bank	…el banco más cercano
…the post office	…el correo/la oficina de correos

…the toilet	…el baño/ aseo/ servicio
Where does the bus to…leave from?	¿De dónde sale el autobús para…?
I'd like a (return) ticket to…	Quisiera un billete (de ida y vuelta) para…
What time does it leave?	¿A qué hora sale ?
(arrive in…)?	(llega a…)?
What is there to eat?	¿Qué hay para comer?

Days of the week

Monday	lunes
Tuesday	martes
Wednesday	miércoles
Thursday	jueves
Friday	viernes
Saturday	sábado
Sunday	domingo

Numbers

1	un/uno/una
2	dos
3	tres
4	cuatro
5	cinco
6	seis
7	siete
8	ocho
9	nueve
10	diez
11	once
12	doce
13	trece
14	catorce
15	quince
16	dieciséis
17	diecisiete
18	dieciocho
19	diecinueve
20	veinte
21	vientiuno
30	treinta
40	cuarenta
50	cincuenta
60	sesenta
70	setenta
80	ochenta
90	noventa
100	cien(to)
200	doscientos
500	quinientos
1000	mil
2000	dos mil

Food and drink

aceitunas	olives
agua	water
ahumados	smoked fish
alioli	garlic mayonnaise
al ajillo	with olive oil and garlic
a la marinera	seafood cooked with garlic, onions and white wine
a la parilla	charcoal-grilled
a la plancha	grilled on a hot plate
a la romana	fried in batter
albóndigas	meatballs
almejas	clams
anchoas	anchovies
arroz	rice
asado	roast
bacalao	cod
berenjena	aubergine/eggplant
bocadillo	bread roll sandwich
boquerones	small, anchovy-like fish, usually served in vinegar
café (con leche)	(white) coffee
calamares	squid
cangrejo	crab
cebolla	onion
cervéza	beer
champiñones	mushrooms
chorizo	spicy sausage
croquetas	croquettes, usually with bits of ham in
cuchara	spoon
cuchillo	knife
dorada	gilt head
empanada	slices of fish/meat pie
ensalada	salad
ensaladilla	Russian salad (diced vegetables in mayonnaise, often with tuna)
fresa	strawberry
gambas	prawns
Hierbas	sweet Ibizan liqueur
hígado	liver
huevos	eggs
jamón serrano	cured ham
jamón de york	regular ham
langostinos	langoustines
lechuga	lettuce
manzana	apple
mejillones	mussels
mojo	garlic dressing available in rojo (spicy "red" version) and "verde" ("green", made with coriander)
naranja	orange
ostras	oysters
pan	bread
patatas alioli	potatoes in garlic mayonnaise
patatas bravas	fried potatoes in a spicy tomato sauce
pimientos	peppers
pimientos de padrón	small peppers, with the odd hot one
piña	pineapple
pisto	assortment of cooked vegetables, similar to ratatouille
plátano	banana
pollo	chicken
pulpo	octopus
queso	cheese
raor	wrase
(Sa) Caleta café	coffee made with brandy and orange peel
salchicha	sausage
setas	oyster mushrooms
sopa	soup
té	tea
tenedor	fork
tomate	tomato
tortilla española	potato omelette
tortilla francesa	plain omelette
vino (blanco/ rosado/tinto)	(white/rosé/red) wine
zarzuela	fish stew
zumo	juice

Glossary

ajuntament town hall
avinguda (avgda) avenue
Baal main Carthaginian deity, "the rider of the clouds", associated with the cult of child sacrifice
baluard bastion
barrio suburb or neighbourhood
cala cove
camí road
campo countryside
can, c'an, cas or c'as house
capella chapel
carrer (c/) street
carretera highway
casament Ibizan farmhouse
castell castle
chiringuito beach café-bar, which usually serves snacks
chupito shot of liquor
Churrigueresque fancifully ornate form of Baroque art, named after its leading exponents, the Spaniard José Churriguera (1650–1723) and his extended family
correu post office
cova cave
Ebusus Roman name for Ibiza Town
Ecotax Balearic environmental tax; abandoned in 2004
Eivissa Catalan name for Ibiza, and Ibiza Town
Eivissenc Catalan dialect spoken in the Pitiuses; it's known as "Ibicenco" in Castilian Spanish

església church
far lighthouse
finca farmhouse
font spring, fountain
Ibosim Carthaginian name for Ibiza Town
illa island
kiosko beach bar or café
mercat market
mirador lookout
museu museum
parada bus stop
parc park
passeig avenue
plaça square
Pitiuses Southern Balearics: Ibiza, Formentera, Espalmador, Espardell, Tagomago and Conillera are the main islands.
platja beach
pou well
puig hill
punta point
riu river
salines salt pans
serra mountain
torre tower
torrent seasonal stream, dried-up river bed
urbanización housing estate
Yebisah Arabic name for Ibiza

ROUGH GUIDES TRAVEL...

Rough Guides are available from good bookstores worldwide. New titles are published every month. Check www.roughguides.com for the latest news.

...MUSIC & REFERENCE

Africa & Middle East
Cape Town
Egypt
The Gambia
Jordan
Kenya
Marrakesh
   DIRECTIONS
Morocco
South Africa, Lesotho & Swaziland
Syria
Tanzania
Tunisia
West Africa
Zanzibar
Zimbabwe

Travel Theme guides
First-Time Around the World
First-Time Asia
First-Time Europe
First-Time Latin America
Skiing & Snowboarding in North America
Travel Online
Travel Health
Walks in London & SE England
Women Travel

Restaurant guides
French Hotels & Restaurants
London
New York
San Francisco

Maps
Algarve
Amsterdam
Andalucia & Costa del Sol

Argentina
Athens
Australia
Baja California
Barcelona
Berlin
Boston
Brittany
Brussels
Chicago
Crete
Croatia
Cuba
Cyprus
Czech Republic
Dominican Republic
Dubai & UAE
Dublin
Egypt
Florence & Siena
Frankfurt
Greece
Guatemala & Belize
Iceland
Ireland
Kenya
Lisbon
London
Los Angeles
Madrid
Mexico
Miami & Key West
Morocco
New York City
New Zealand
Northern Spain
Paris
Peru
Portugal
Prague
Rome
San Francisco
Sicily
South Africa
South India
Sri Lanka
Tenerife
Thailand
Toronto

Trinidad & Tobago
Tuscany
Venice
Washington DC
Yucatán Peninsula

Dictionary Phrasebooks
Czech
Dutch
Egyptian Arabic
European Languages (Czech, French, German, Greek, Italian, Portuguese, Spanish)
French
German
Greek
Hindi & Urdu
Hungarian
Indonesian
Italian
Japanese
Mandarin Chinese
Mexican Spanish
Polish
Portuguese
Russian
Spanish
Swahili
Thai
Turkish
Vietnamese

Music Guides
The Beatles
Bob Dylan
Cult Pop
Classical Music
Country Music
Elvis
Hip Hop
House
Irish Music
Jazz
Music USA
Opera

Reggae
Rock
Techno
World Music (2 vols)

History Guides
China
Egypt
England
France
India
Islam
Italy
Spain
USA

Reference Guides
Books for Teenagers
Children's Books, 0–5
Children's Books, 5–11
Cult Fiction
Cult Football
Cult Movies
Cult TV
Ethical Shopping
Formula 1
The iPod, iTunes & Music Online
The Internet
Internet Radio
James Bond
Kids' Movies
Lord of the Rings
Muhammed Ali
Man Utd
Personal Computers
Pregnancy & Birth
Shakespeare
Superheroes
Unexplained Phenomena
The Universe
Videogaming
Weather
Website Directory

Also! More than 120 Rough Guide music CDs are available from all good book and record stores. Listen in at www.worldmusic.net

small print & **Index**

A Rough Guide to Rough Guides

Ibiza DIRECTIONS is published by Rough Guides. The first *Rough Guide to Greece*, published in 1982, was a student scheme that became a publishing phenomenon. The immediate success of the book – with numerous reprints and a Thomas Cook prize shortlisting – spawned a series that rapidly covered dozens of destinations. Rough Guides had a ready market among low-budget backpackers, but soon also acquired a much broader and older readership that relished Rough Guides' wit and inquisitiveness as much as their enthusiastic, critical approach. Everyone wants value for money, but not at any price. Rough Guides soon began supplementing the "rougher" information about hostels and low-budget listings with the kind of detail on restaurants and quality hotels that independent-minded visitors on any budget might expect, whether on business in New York or trekking in Thailand. These days the guides offer recommendations from shoestring to luxury and cover a large number of destinations around the globe, including almost every country in the Americas and Europe, more than half of Africa and most of Asia and Australasia. Rough Guides now publish:

- Travel guides to more than 200 worldwide destinations
- Dictionary phrasebooks to 22 major languages
- Maps printed on rip-proof and waterproof Polyart™ paper
- Music guides running the gamut from Opera to Elvis
- Reference books on topics as diverse as the Weather and Shakespeare
- World Music CDs in association with World Music Network

Visit **www.roughguides.com** to see our latest publications.

Publishing information

This 1st edition published June 2005 by
Rough Guides Ltd, 80 Strand, London WC2R 0RL.
345 Hudson St, 4th Floor, New York, NY 10014, USA.

Distributed by the Penguin Group
Penguin Books Ltd, 80 Strand, London WC2R 0RL.
Penguin Group (USA), 375 Hudson Street, NY 10014, USA.
Penguin Group (Australia), 250 Camberwell Road, Camberwell, Victoria 3124, Australia.
Penguin Group (Canada), 10 Alcorn Avenue, Toronto, ON M4V 1E4, Canada.
Penguin Group (New Zealand), Cnr Rosedale and Airborne Roads, Albany, Auckland, New Zealand.
Typeset in Bembo and Helvetica to an original design by Henry Iles.
Printed and bound in China .

208pp includes index

A catalogue record for this book is available from the British Library.

ISBN 1-84353-420-7

The publishers and authors have done their best to ensure the accuracy and currency of all the information in **Ibiza DIRECTIONS**, however, they can accept no responsibility for any loss, injury, or inconvenience sustained by any traveller as a result of information or advice contained in the guide.

1   3   5   7   9   8   6   4   2

Help us update

We've gone to a lot of effort to ensure that the first edition of **Ibiza DIRECTIONS** is accurate and up-to-date. However, things change – places get "discovered", opening hours are notoriously fickle, restaurants and rooms raise prices or lower standards. If you feel we've got it wrong or left something out, we'd like to know, and if you can remember the address, the price, the phone number, so much the better.

We'll credit all contributions, and send a copy of the next edition (or any other DIRECTIONS guide or Rough Guide if you prefer) for the best letters. Everyone who writes to us and isn't already a subscriber will receive a copy of our full-colour thrice-yearly newsletter. Please mark letters: "**Ibiza DIRECTIONS Update**" and send to: Rough Guides, 80 Strand, London WC2R 0RL, or Rough Guides, 4th Floor, 345 Hudson St, New York, NY 10014. Or send an email to **mail@roughguides.com**.
Have your questions answered and tell others about your trip at **www.roughguides.atinfopop.com**.

Rough Guide credits

Text editor: Sally Schafer
Layout: Dan May
Photography: Demetrio Carrasco
Cartography: Rajesh Mishra, Ed Wright
Picture editor: Jj Luck

Proofreader: David Price
Production: Julia Bovis
Design: Henry Iles
Cover design: Louise Boulton and Chloë Roberts

The author

Author of the Rough Guide to Guatemala and contributor to the Rough Guides to Central America and Spain, **Iain Stewart** first took his bucket and spade to the Balearics as a toddler and has been returning regularly ever since. He lives in Brighton.

Acknowledgements

I'd like to acknowledge the work of my editor Sally Schafer, whose thorough, unflappable approach contributed greatly to this edition. In Ibiza thanks to Martin Davies for his all-round Ibiza expertise, Enrique Moreno, Andy and Chrissie Wilson and Senyor Antoni Roselló. It was great to have my family – Fee, Louis and Monty, Dave and Simone, Jan and Betty, Susan and Aubs – as well as Andy and Becky Felstead along for the ride too.

Readers' letters

David and Jacky Boulton, Terri Wagner Cooper, Amanda Crook, Fiona Day, Eri Gideon, Pete Kilby, Tim Payne, George Rhone, Susan Rosenberg, Sebastian Schroeder, George Serna, Julia Sheraton, Joyce Simson, Noel C. Sullivan, Pilar Webb.

Photo credits

All images © Rough Guides except the following:

Front cover picture: Es Vedrà © Demon Library
Back cover picture: Clubbing scene © Demon Library

p.2 Ibiza Town and harbour © Firecrest/Robert Harding
p.7 Dalt Vila © Stone/Getty
p.10 Salines saltpans © Iain Stewart
p.12 Can Lluc © Iain Stewart
p.13 Es Cucons © Iain Stewart
p.15 Space © Space
p.16 Beach fun © Iain Stewart

p.19 Cala Salada © Iain Stewart
p.19 Benirràs © Simon Lloyd
p.21 El Secreto de Baltasar © Iain Stewart
p.22 Gusto © Iain Stewart
p.28 Hippodrome market © Iain Stewart
p.35 Platja Codolar © Iain Stewart
p.38 Yoga retreat © Simon Lloyd
p.40 Defence tower, southern Ibiza © Iain Stewart
p.41 Atlantis © Iain Stewart
p.44 Defence tower, eastern Ibiza © Iain Stewart
p.50 Es Torrent © Rainer Jahns/Alamy
p.144 Space © Space

Index

Maps are marked in colour